Praise for *One Team, One Score*

Great leaders invest in their teams through communication, coaching, and caring. *One Team One Score* by Dr. Ann Marie Gorczyca is a blueprint for leadership development and a foundation for creating the courage necessary to maintain your practice's team cultural standard of optimism and excellence.

–Jon Gordon, 14x best-selling author
Author of *The Energy Bus* and *The Energy Bus for Kids*

Dr. Ann Marie Gorczyca is a gift to the dental profession. Her book, *One Team One Score*, describes the essence of leadership and teamwork including how to build a great culture of productivity, appreciation, and open communication. I'd recommend that every dental professional, and every small business leader for that matter, read this book and take notes!

–Amy Hiett, Executive Coach, Co-founder of the Table Group

The number-one job of a business owner is to lead their team toward a specific vision. As a consultant, I truly believe nothing will ruin a team faster than a leader tolerating undesirable behaviors. Dr. Gorczyca shares decades of experience leading her own team, lessons learned, and teamwork actions which work. *One Team One Score* provides insight which will help you lead a winning team.

–Dino Watt, CEO Dino Watt Consulting
Author of *Hire & Fire Like a Boss*

One Team One Score will help you and your team build both leadership and teamwork success. Dr. Ann Marie Gorczyca has lived and breathed leadership, teamwork, and collaboration experiences. She lays out methods in her book which can be used to lead, build, and maintain an excellent office team culture. *One Team One Score* is a remarkable book with useful strategies, both of which I highly recommend.

–Michelle Shimmin, CEO, Consultant, Business Analyst
Shimmin Consulting Practice Management

This may just be the most important book released in dentistry in the last ten years! Here's why. With the growing competition among dentists globally, the failure or success of dental practices relies much more on the leadership of the practitioner than their technical skills. And leadership is something that is virtually never covered in any dental school curriculum internationally. Unlike so many other aspects of running a dental practice that can be effectively outsourced—marketing, IT, accounting, etc.—leadership cannot. If leadership at the practice is not going well, the practice will fail to thrive. What is particularly refreshing about this book is that the steps toward leadership outlined by the author are eminently achievable. Dr. Ann Marie Gorczyca has done an amazing job at turning the complex into the simple, with a proven system that will make every dental practice owner a better leader. *One Team One Score* is essential reading for any dental practice owner with aspirations of running a successful and stress-free practice.

–Angus Pryor, Founder/CEO, Dental Marketing Solutions
Author of *The Dental Practice Profit System*

One Team One Score will give you the tools and courage to become an effective leader and create a winning team. It is a must-read for dentists, health professionals, and team leaders in the industry. It is a privilege to share in Ann Marie's genuine experience through the lens of her new book *One Team One Score.*

–Sahar Jaffrey, DDS, MS, Pediatric Dentist
Past President of the Contra Costa Dental Society

Dr. Ann Marie Gorczyca's book *One Team One Score* provides dental practice owners, and all dentists, a valuable resource for handling all-too-common employment pitfalls. With useful case studies and tips, this book serves as a helpful resource, at a time when dental employment disputes and related lawsuits only seem to be on the rise. As the owner of her own dental practice, Dr. Ann Marie Gorczyca has the experience to recognize and discuss these critical issues that all owners and prospective dental practice owners should understand and appreciate. *One Team One Score* is an important contribution to the business of dentistry.

–Peter Finn, Attorney
J Supple Law

Few topics may be as undervalued as leadership and team culture. With no data to mind or specific goals to achieve, too many small business owners in all disciplines neglect this sometimes-uncomfortable topic at their own peril. Poor leadership and dysfunctional team culture can be a troublesome combination, and difficult to uncover, causing problems for the entire business.

With her customary clarity honed over multiple books and journal articles, Dr. Ann Marie Gorczyca demystifies the subject of leadership and teamwork with concrete examples and actions any dentist or orthodontist can apply to their own practice. Whether you are a seasoned practitioner or just starting on your professional journey, *One Team One Score* is so packed with pearls of wisdom that here, you will find something to benefit your own business and life.

–Phil Vogels, MBA
Vice President, Journal of Clinical Orthodontics

Foreword by Bernie Stoltz

One Team, One
SCORE

Leadership and Teamwork
for a Successful Dental Practice

DR. ANN MARIE GORCZYCA

AUTHORITY
PUBLISHING

ONE TEAM, ONE SCORE
Leadership and Teamwork for a Successful Dental Practice
by Ann Marie Gorczyca

MED016090 – Medical: Dentistry - Practice Management
MED016000 – Medical: Dentistry – General
BUS043000 – Business & Economics: Marketing - General

ISBN: 979-8-88636-032-5 (paperback)
ISBN: 979-8-88636-022-6 (hardcover)
ISBN: 979-8-88636-023-3 (ebook)

Cover design by
Lewis Agrell

Printed in the United States of America

Authority Publishing
13389 Folsom Blvd #300-256
Folsom, CA 95630
800-877-1097
www.AuthorityPublishing.com

DEDICATIONS

To the Northern California Angle Society of Orthodontists:
Thank you for the opportunity to be your president from
2021 to 2023.

To all the outstanding team members of Gorczyca Orthodontics,
past and present, especially
Lyndsay, Jessica, Madison, Leona, and Jolene.
Thank you for the privilege of working with you.

CONTENTS

FOREWORD

In her book *One Team, One Score,* Dr. Ann Marie Gorczyca brings to life the essential qualities of leaders—courage, integrity, preparation, decisiveness, teamwork, and clarity. At Fortune Management, we are huge advocates of the "modeling success" process and learning from great leaders. As a fellow optimist, I am especially cheered by Ann Marie's advice to "stay persistently positive." By communicating passion and reaching people on an emotional level, as a leader, you develop your team to become partners in meaningful and purposeful work. Dr. Gorczyca demonstrated that leaders have the capacity to envision and create a better future. Great leaders see the best in people. A truly great leader sees more in their people than they see in themselves while inspiring them to become even greater.

Dr. Gorczyca understands that the CEO of the dental practice is the culture keeper. The leader leads by example, while holding people accountable for consistent standards of excellence. Leaders make decisions and take a stand while "leaning into discomfort" to tackle problems head-on. The doctor, CEO, or president can't do it all themselves. *One Team, One Score* emphasizes the importance of leaders creating other leaders. Ann Marie describes this as co-elevation. I call it creating win-win relationships.

At Fortune Management, we understand the importance of being coachable and open to improvement. We wholeheartedly agree with Ann Marie that a key component of growing people, and your practice, involves a commitment to Constant And Never-Ending Improvement (CANI). When the whole team has this growth mindset, and master problems together, they become an unstoppable team.

One Team, One Score is a must-have guide giving dentists the skills they need to become a great leader and to create a winning team.

–Bernie Stoltz, CEO, Fortune Management
Author of *The Fortune Recipe*

INTRODUCTION

Either write something worth reading or
do something worth writing.
–Benjamin Franklin

T eam: An alignment of people working together to achieve a result. Whether you're part of a dental office, dental society, symphony orchestra, or tennis team, your efforts in leadership, teamwork, and collaboration result in your overall performance success. The common goal of a leader and a team is to work together. Begin your leadership journey by using the word "We."

In the dental office, we bring together people of various backgrounds to work as one unified team. This is no small task. It is even more difficult in a volunteer organization where everyone is a professional, has an ego, and the team changes every few years. All must be engaged in the working relationship.

As a dentist, you have taken the risks of practice ownership. With this, you have earned the right of leadership. In the professional organization, the leader is often the one with the longest tenure, the biggest contributor, or the loudest politician.

Effective leadership presents many challenges. But to run a successful dental office, the owner must assume the lead or hire someone else who will. Otherwise, the strongest personality on your team, with the loudest voice and most dominant personality, will take over. The team's job is to achieve specific outcomes. Ultimately, your ability to coach your team will determine everyone's success.

This book was written to help you hone your personal leadership and teamwork skills. Beyond the dental practice, this book can also help you with the challenges presented by your professional volunteer organization.

There may be times when as leader, you might feel like giving up. You cannot. Otherwise, what is the alternative? To be an employee of a corporation without freedom or equity? To abdicate responsibility as leader or lose opportunities to participate in needed change? I hope that this book will help you and carry you through with courage, communication, and candor.

Too many dentists "sell out" on their own dental practice management leadership. Not mastering the skills of leadership and teamwork might create the necessity to sell your life's work, your practice, to a dental service organization (DSO). This short-term gain does not serve a good long-term result. It may not result in the personal or financial fulfillment that you desire or anticipate.

If you are serving your dental society as leader or officer, you are setting an example for future leaders. You want that example to be good, displaying dedication, strength, courage, ethics, and inclusion. You cannot abdicate your responsibilities and go back on your commitment, expecting others would want to follow.

I hope that every dentist is successful. Dentists must lead themselves before they start strategizing ideal organizational behavior and performance outcomes for others. Once mastery over self is achieved, the quest then turns to modelling and implementing optimal group dynamics.

As dentists we are given the opportunity of equity and freedom in the running of our offices. If we don't run our business well, we give up the incredible gifts of effective dental practice management and the benefits of serving others, including coworkers, patients, and colleagues.

Leading a Team

Don't find fault, find a remedy.

–Henry Ford

Leading and maintaining a successful dental practice is challenging. Just when you have the perfect team, someone will retire, move away, or be out on maternity leave. Or, all three could happen at the same time! It will be your job to deal with the everyday challenges of practice management for your entire career.

When I was a student at the Harvard School of Dental Medicine, I had the opportunity to study at Harvard School of Public Health in the Department of Health Management and Policy. Although I learned many valuable business management skills there, no lectures on leadership or teamwork were offered at that time. It was during the time I spent there, however, that I had my first valuable *leadership* opportunity.

During the years 1987 to 1988, I had the privilege of serving as the chairperson of the board of directors of the Longwood Symphony Orchestra, a symphony in which I was principal flutist for five years. This organization had many esteemed people on the board during that time, including a trumpet player who was dean of the Harvard School of Public Health, Harvey Feinberg, and Harvard School of Dental Medicine professor and head of the Department of Public Health Dentistry, Dr. Chester Douglass, then a member of the Tanglewood Festival Summer Chorus. Other members were esteemed professionals from the Longwood Medical Community and administrative professionals from the hospital community.

Holding this position as chairman of the board was an initiation. I learned how to run a meeting guided by Rules of Order, with an agenda, discussing tough issues like firing the conductor, and starting and ending the meeting on time. We raised money and had a balanced budget. The meetings were effective and orderly.

I was fortunate at that time to have an excellent mentor on the board of directors of the symphony, Carol Winck, the president of the Longwood Symphony, an epidemiologist and oboist. She would often pull me aside, saying, "You can't get emotional," or "Stay objective." I am happy to report that the governance of the Longwood Symphony Orchestra remains strong to this day.

Serving the board of a dental society was a different experience. Microaggressions prevailed, members quit and threatened to quit, meeting agendas were interrupted, meetings occasionally ran for three and a half hours as members pontificated, and policy and procedures were outdated and not followed. We had a lot of work to do!

Today we use American Institute of Parliamentarians Standard Code of Parliamentary Procedure (2012) for board of directors' meetings, but the rules and practices are the same. We are trying to move in a positive direction, but we have much to accomplish in dentistry in the area of ideal organization behavior, especially in the areas of equity, kindness, empathy, and inclusion.

I first experienced true *teamwork* as a member of the San Francisco City College tennis team during 1995–1997. It was here that I learned that being on a team can be one of the best experiences of your life. There can also be trying situations and difficult interpersonal personality issues. At these times, team alignment is tested. I am grateful to the leadership of our coach, Mary Graber, for all the valuable teamwork and leadership lessons she taught me and everyone on the team.

When I started teaching at the University of the Pacific Arthur A. Dugoni School of Dentistry, we added a teamwork lecture to our practice management course. It was not until writing this book that I added the leadership portion to this lecture, realizing after thirty-two years in practice and organizational service just how important true leadership skills are to all of our dental organizations, and how badly an objective understanding of this topic is needed. I now understand that without acceptance of strong leadership, egos can change teamwork to anarchy.

I have also served on orthodontic department faculties and witnessed how egos can destroy leadership and teamwork. It's easy to destroy but very hard to build. I am grateful that in my early career, I had the opportunity to work with a great leader in dentistry, Dr. Robert Boyd, at both UCSF and University of the Pacific Dental School. Dr. Boyd is a good man and an effective leader, loved by all who served with him. I am grateful for his dedication and service to the orthodontic profession.

I have witnessed organizational dysfunction in the form of large boards and ineffective committees. There's lot of work to be done by dentists in the leadership and teamwork arenas if we expect our societies and specialties to continue to thrive.

In the real world of dental practice management, leadership and teamwork are two seldom-mentioned but necessary subjects that every dentist needs to master in order to thrive. This book will add to your insight into these two areas.

A Leadership Awakening

> *Lead, follow, or get out of the way.*
>
> –Lee Iacocca

In 2021, I became the first woman president of the Northern California Angle Society of Orthodontists. This twenty-six-year journey was a struggle for me from start to finish. As I faced my most difficult challenges, I was determined to learn all I could about leadership and teamwork.

I started my term with the teamwork goals of Alan Mulally. I thought that if they worked for him at Ford Motor Company, they could work for me. Some appreciated my enthusiasm for leadership and teamwork. Some did not. Every leader's style will be different. I was focused on clarity of purpose and goals for the organization. I looked for an experienced mentor. I am grateful to Dr. Gary Baughman, past president of the Angle Society, Pacific Coast Society of Orthodontists, and Parliamentarian for the American Association of Orthodontists, and his lovely wife, Carol, for meeting with me to discuss goals and leadership challenges.

I hired a leadership coach from the Table Group consulting company of Patrick Lencioni, pioneer of the organizational health movement and best-selling author of twelve teamwork and leadership books, including *The Five Dysfunctions of a Team, The Advantage,* and *The Ideal Team Player.* I am eternally grateful to Amy Hiett, the leadership coach from the Table Group, for her support and consultations during my time of leadership service.

The themes of this book are *leadership, teamwork,* and *collaboration.* Teamwork is an activity in which every office member participates, especially the doctor. The doctor is not an equal member of the team and serves the best interests of the team doing whatever needs to be done. Leading the office team is the highest priority. In this leadership quest, the leader is also a servant.

A well-aligned team is one of the greatest joys in dentistry and in life. When your team takes excellent care of your patients while working well together, they make success for everyone possible and enjoyable. Dentistry, after all, is a business dependent upon service by an excellent team. As dental professionals, we must never lose sight that a happy team leads to happy patients, and ultimately, to a happy doctor. Once achieved, you've got it made.

As dentists, we want to get leadership right. This will take courage, communication, and candor, as well as vision, focus, and a willing team. Included in this book are tips and exercises that can help you with leadership and teamwork on your personal journey to success. I hope that you will enjoy the activities and discussions in this book. Here's to leveraging leadership, teamwork, and collaboration for success. Now, let's get started!

HOW TO USE THIS BOOK

Leadership is the capacity to translate vision into reality.
–Warren G. Bennis

Leadership, teamwork, and collaboration are a combination of actions integrated to organizational success. When all of these processes run seamlessly, without stress or effort, you are practicing in management heaven.

Actions for consideration in the organizational behavior of your business are therefore divided into three main categories:

1. Leadership—accepting your role and having the courage to step forward;
2. Teamwork—creating an energized, cohesive working group; and
3. Collaboration—creating momentum for results and success.

Once you have mastered these three areas of dental practice management, your days will be filled with satisfaction.

This book outlines exercises and tips to help you be the leader you need to be to run your dental practice, create an effective team, streamline your dental organization, and keep everyone working together toward common goals. Use these tactics to fill in your own "to do" list of action items. A sample template, as well as a blank template that you can complete and share with your team, is included at the back of the book.

PART ONE

LEADERSHIP

The first responsibility of a leader is to define reality.
The last is to say thank you.
In between, the leader is a servant.

–Max DePree

Whomever you lead, whether it is your dental office team, a society of volunteers, a board of directors, or even your family, leadership is about your people. Leadership is not a title, it is action. Leaders rise or are appointed to bring about change and get things done. Simply put, a leader gets the mission accomplished by turning a shared vision into a reality.

Mahatma Gandhi and Martin Luther King, Jr. were incredible leaders, yet they had no official position or title. Whoever puts in the hours organizing to achieve the mission is a leader. Even if you have never been given the title, you may be a leader just by your passion and dedication to a cause. Your dental office has a team of customer service leaders. Your team is empowered to make your patients happy. The people who serve your organization are leaders through their volunteerism. Those who take action are displaying their leadership.

Creating a leadership- and teamwork-centered culture of working together is the ultimate goal for achieving organizational success. If leadership is change, management is the actions of making that change. Both are necessary in the business environment.

Strong leadership with weak management or weak leadership with strong management won't work. Strong management seldom exists with weak leadership or a weak team. Once you understand the difference, you can begin the work necessary to provide both. Hopefully, during your journey of leadership and teamwork, you will create a collaborative team-work structure to ensure the success of your office or organization.

Chapter 1

CALL

Only three things happen naturally in organizations:
friction, confusion, and underperformance.
Everything else requires leadership.

–Peter Drucker

C ongratulations! You have accepted the call to leadership. By buying this book, reading it, and working to improve your leadership skills, you will learn what others have found only by trial and error.

Leadership is not for the faint of heart. It is not a title. It requires courage, communication, and candor about what changes are needed and what issues need to be resolved. A true leader creates change.

If you are the leader, the success of your team rests on your shoulders. Perhaps you are the leader of your dental organization. You might be thinking, *Where do I start?* Your passion and dedication have led you to this place. Ask yourself, "What change can I make for a better future for those whom I lead?"

Leadership is change. When you think of great leaders throughout history, such as Gandhi, Martin Luther King, Jr., Abraham Lincoln, or even Jesus Christ, you remember them as unstoppable people who had a cause and conviction.

Exceptional leadership starts with acceptance of the role of leader. By the mere fact that you made a decision to own a dental practice or took on a leadership position in your society, you have accepted the call to leadership. You have taken the first step. That in itself gives you the title of CEO or leader. Now, what can you do to become an exceptional leader?

THREE STEPS TO LEADERSHIP

> *Teamwork simply stated is less me and more we.*
> –Anonymous

STEP ONE: USE THE WORD "WE"

Who calls the team together? Who holds the team together? Who makes the decisions for the strongest team? The leader.

Just like the coach of a winning Super Bowl team, as a business owner, your goal is to build the best, strongest, and most winning team possible. This will take courage, good hiring decisions, candor, and leadership.

STEP TWO: CLARIFY GOALS AND ISSUES

Why do teams have coaches? To clarify what is most important, identify problems and find solutions, and lead the team toward success. The leader encourages the team to do great work together. The vision and plan is presented by the leader. The leader helps to make the team a high-performing group working toward their common goal.

This is the primary job of a leader: to define the mission. The leader leads by example. There will always be challenges running a dental practice. As the years pass, employees will come and go, and the team will remain in a state of evolution. One thing that will not change, *you* as the owner of your practice and leader of your dental team.

STEP THREE: SURROUND YOURSELF WITH "A" PLAYERS

Face it, you cannot run your dental practice alone. You need a great team. As the leader, put your ego aside and ask for help. Everyone needs to pitch in. You want to recruit and work only with all players who bring their "A" game to work every day.

On a team, everyone needs to speak the truth, share the goals, and have each other's backs. You cannot afford to have a disengaged team member or one person who sabotages the whole. Everyone needs to be aligned on the goals and work together. It is your job as the leader, coach, or manager to make this happen.

To start your leadership journey, let's review different forms of leadership. What is your leadership style?

FOUR FORMS OF LEADERSHIP

Leadership and learning are indispensable to each other.
–John F. Kennedy

There are four forms of leadership: authoritative, bureaucratic, democratic, and laissez-faire. Let's take a closer look at each.

AUTHORITATIVE LEADERSHIP

Authoritative leadership has a single leader doing what they would like to do. It could be the director of a dental study club. This club has no board of directors or member input on how it is run. There are no votes, there is no input, and there is very little, if any, opportunity for leadership by the members.

In an organization such as this, you will need to decide if the culture of the group is right for you. As a dental professional, you must decide if the code of conduct lives up to your standards and if you want to be part of this group.

When it comes to countries under authoritative leadership, we call it a dictatorship. Someone or some group has total control. Citizens abide.

BUREAUCRATIC LEADERSHIP

Bureaucratic leadership has a hierarchy of power. This could describe a dental school where someone has become the dean through tenure. Many dental societies might also be considered to be bureaucratic. Leadership paths involve rising through the ranks in a systematic fashion based on service and tenure.

Perhaps there is a designated ascension in your dental organization that, once started, the membership's chair becomes secretary, the secretary becomes treasurer, the treasurer becomes vice president, and the vice president becomes president. There may be oversight by a board of directors.

For the American Dental Association (ADA) and other dental societies, bureaucratic leadership roles are defined by a plan in the Organizational Bylaws. There is a stated Code of Professional Conduct and Ethics set forth by the organization and the Dental Practice Act.

Organizational bureaucracy is not all bad. In some cases, it can build loyalty and reward members for dedication over the years. If the rules are known, fair, and maintained, surprises and misunderstandings can be prevented.

DEMOCRATIC LEADERSHIP

Although the United States is a constitutional republic, democratic processes when implemented fairly have been deemed the best leadership style for "liberty and justice for all." Democracy theoretically gives everyone a voice and an opportunity for leadership. However, at times it is messy. It can also be full of surprises.

In our dental offices, although not a true democracy, we aspire to have everyone's voice heard and opinion counted, so that we can make the best overall decision and chart the optimal future course for the team and doctor. We want our team members engaged, informed, and committed to our office decisions, knowing that the ultimate decisions have been made fairly. The owner of a dental office can take a vote and consider the input of the entire team.

In the end, however, the owner of the dental office will make the final decision. It is his or her own financial risk and assets on the line. In this regard, a dental office is not a true democracy. The CEO leads by "executive order," while following state and federal employment laws, including human resource (HR) codes.

LAISSEZ-FAIRE LEADERSHIP

Laissez-faire leadership is the worst leadership form of all. Essentially, it is no leadership. It results in a free-for-all. There is very little teamwork. Most often, the loudest voice wins.

Many professional organizations and dental offices suffer from laissez-faire leadership. There is no framework of acceptable behavior. In the absence of leadership, bad things can happen. Bullying triumphs. A hostile work environment prevails. Management systems become disorganized or ignored. Anarchy occurs. Success is undefined and slips away.

LEARN FROM SUCCESSFUL LEADERS

> *The pessimist complains about the wind.*
> *The optimist expects it to change.*
> *The leader adjusts the sails.*
> –John C. Maxwell

I searched to find the greatest living American business leaders from whom we can learn. One name repeatedly came up: Alan Mulally, former CEO of Ford Motor Company.

In the book, *American Icon: Alan Mulally and the Fight to Save Ford Motor Company,* author Bryce G. Hoffman describes the day Mr. Mulally took the plane home after visiting Ford to consider becoming CEO. Mulally recognized that Ford's culture needed help, as it was inbred with many ineffective relatives of Henry Ford in leadership or management positions. Mulally knew that he was the right person to create change.

For clarity, he first listed his two goals: (1) make the best cars in the world; and (2) create profitable growth for all. Next, he listed his four areas of improvement strategy, his four Ps: performance, product, process, and people. Lastly, he listed the key metrics which he would track in his weekly business plan review meeting to build team engagement, create momentum, and improve performance.

When he was done with his organized plan, he wrote, **"Wow! What fun!"**

Alan Mulally's style of leadership—enthusiasm, organization, high energy, and fun—was his key to success. Viewing him on YouTube, Mulally looks relaxed and appealing. He's likeable. It is immediately apparent that he is cool, calm, and collected, and he loves what he does. He makes you think, "I'd love to work with that guy!"

What's your leadership persona? Is it enthusiastic? Or, is it stressed-out? I assure you that enthusiasm works best. Learn to love leadership and your style will be one of confidence and enjoyment.

Yes, it can be lonely being the leader. It can also be fun. So, go for it! Take center stage and let it rip! Make your leadership style a positive one that others will want to follow.

Alan Mulally was able to pull off one of the greatest turnarounds in business history. He led Ford Motor Company from the brink of bankruptcy to being one of the most profitable automakers in the world. How did he do it?

Mulally's organizational teamwork requirements are contained in the book *Working Together: 12 Principles for Achieving Excellence in Managing Projects, Teams, and Organizations* by James P. Lewis. In the foreword to this book, Mulally discusses how his "working together" principles were key to his leadership and teamwork successes. For those who want to try them in their own dental office or society, here are twelve principles for success of Alan Mulally:

Twelve Principles for Working Together

1. *Have a compelling vision.*
2. *Everyone's included.*
3. *There's one plan.*
4. *Know the clear performance goals.*
5. *Present facts and data.*
6. *Respect, listen, and help each other.*
7. *Whining is OK—occasionally, if you present a solution.*
8. *Have emotional resilience.*
9. *Maintain a "find a way, propose a plan" positive attitude.*
10. *You can't manage a secret.*
11. *Have fun! Enjoy the journey and each other.*
12. *Working together provides a framework to live a life you can be proud of.*

This is how we can lead as well. I printed these twelve principles on orange cards for team members both in my office and at our society.

Author James P. Lewis states that he believes Mulally's principles of teamwork success are character-based. Through these principles, the character of each team member who follows them is built. For Mulally, these principles were so important that he would begin each weekly team meeting by reviewing them.

A Leader Gives Everyone a Voice

Being heard is so close to being loved that for the average person, they are almost indistinguishable.
—David Augsburger

We have one rule at our team meetings: everyone gives a report with the opportunity to speak. We want to hear from each team member because words matter, their work matters, they matter. Everyone present at the meeting is an integral, included part of the team, with a distinct voice. This is where they belong.

No meeting can end before everyone shares input. Underlying all of this is a leader who seeks out connection and makes sure that all are heard.

To get team engagement flowing, ask these three simple questions:

1. ***What do you like most about our office?***
2. ***What do you like least about our office?***
3. ***What would you change?***

Your team's feedback will lead to improvement changes. When made from this list of suggestions, give credit to the idea's originator, your team, and individual team members.

This exercise sends the message, "You help make our office great." It also reinforces the message, "We are all in this together." This feedback will lead to improvement changes.

A Leader Has Passion for the Cause

Be strong enough to stand alone,
smart enough to know when you need help,
and brave enough to ask for it.
—Ziad K. Abdelnour

Think of great leaders: Gandhi, Mandela, Churchill, John Paul II, or maybe even Joan of Arc. These were daring people. They were outspoken. They had passion. They had a cause. They took action and they inspired others.

Leaders are change agents. Leaders go first and function on the edge of consensus. Leaders might not even be understood for what they are doing. But in the end, their actions will lead others to take action, resulting in change.

It is not a title, position, or elected office that makes one a leader. It is not an appointment of a nomination committee. It is action, influence, and results.

A leader can be charismatic or transformational in their expression of what needs to be done. Either way, it is necessary to communicate your vision to your team with passion so that others can get excited about the plan and take action to join it.

You can't fake leadership. In communicating your vision as leader, speak from the heart and be your authentic self.

A Leader Asks Questions to Learn More

Jeff Polzer, a Harvard Business School professor who studies organizational behavior, states there are two critical moments that happen in a group's life:

1. The first vulnerability; and
2. The first disagreement.

In these critical moments, the group is either divided as independently strong individuals, or becomes a group working together. It is at these critical defensive times that it is best for a teamwork-oriented leader to ask:

> *"Why?"*
> *"Please tell me more."*
> *"Why don't you agree?"*
> *"I'm curious about your conclusion. Let's talk about this more."*

Teamwork is about mutual discovery. There will be disagreements. It is at these difficult times that the leader must remember that their job is to reveal the truths and connections that will enable cooperation.

A Great Leader Listens

> *Listen! Or your tongue will make you deaf.*
> —Cherokee saying

Listening is invisible and gets no attention. There are no awards for effective listeners. Listening is leading by respect. In his book, *Communicate or Die: Getting Results Through Speaking and Listening,* global leadership coach Thomas D. Zweifel, PhD presents the Matterhorn of masterful listening.

At the bottom of this pyramid is ignoring and pretending, which is what most ineffective leaders do. Ignoring is absence of listening. Pretending is appearing to listen when you're really not.

Next is controlling and projecting. These leaders cut people off from speaking, not even letting them complete their sentence. They think that they know what the person is going to say. They influence what the speaker is attempting to say through body language, facial expressions, smirks, eye-rolling, and sounds. Projecting is listening through the filter of your own beliefs. Hearing only what you want to hear, you are projecting that you know it all.

Effective leaders listen effectively by respecting and empathizing. By respecting, leaders hear the content of what is actually being said. This is the first step of true leadership. Input and ideas flow to the leader from which success can be bred. By empathizing, the leader listens for the speaker's intention. The leader then learns to truly know and understand the speaker. A relationship and trust are developed.

The highest levels of listening are generating and mastery. The listener listens for the speaker's brilliance. They are anticipating the gold that results from a conversation based on active listening.

A LEADER IS VULNERABLE

> *A leader, first and foremost, is human.*
> *Only when we have the strength to show our vulnerability*
> *can we truly lead.*
> –Simon Sinek

As leader, don't be afraid to say, "I messed up" and be vulnerable. In return, you are giving your team the confidence needed to also be vulnerable. It is in situations when team members are not comfortable being open that they cover up their weaknesses and mistakes.

We can all use help with our weaknesses. By the leader expressing their own need for help, they make the office a safe place for others to ask for assistance. Try these words: *"I need help."* Similarly, volunteer to help your team. Simply state: *"Tell me what you want, and I'll help you."*

Vulnerability is the most basic building block of trust. In order for vulnerability to exist in a relationship, it must exist in both directions. It's easy for a leader to issue commands and seem bossy. A better approach would be to facilitate open lines of communication:

"Anybody have any good ideas?"

In a dental office, we're all vulnerable. None of us can do it all on our own. Everyone contributes. Everyone is needed. Everyone counts.

A Leader Shows Appreciation

*Sixty-four percent of Americans who leave their jobs
say they do so because they don't feel appreciated.*
–US Department of Labor

In April 2021, I showed appreciation to an outstanding member of my team, Lyndsay. She accomplished the unimaginable: she got our thirty, sixty, and ninety-plus days accounts receivable down to zero money owed. I consider this a *huge* accomplishment, never done before, and something that I have personally worked on for over thirty years.

When Lyndsay proudly showed me her report, I told her I would like to buy her a gift, perhaps a bottle of champagne to celebrate. She said, "I don't drink."

I asked, "What would you like then?"

She said, "Chips."

In preparation for my next day's team meeting, I visited the grocery store, bought a huge gift bag, and filled it with every conceivable type of chip. I also added dip, soft drinks, and Reese's peanut butter cups. I included a card, stating, "You put the Awe in Awesome, the Wonder in Wonderful, the Extra in Extraordinary!" As a team, we celebrated Lyndsay and her success with what she enjoyed.

I could immediately feel the inspiration that the other team members got from Lyndsay's achievement. Others started volunteering to begin their own projects that we had discussed. Everyone was excited. At the end of the day, we took a team photo, and I told every patient that day that this was one of the happiest days in our practice because of what an amazing job Lyndsay had done. I had Lyndsay sign her Zero A/R sheet and I placed a gold seal of excellence on it. I framed it and put it up on my office "Wall of Fame." Lyndsay is our new Queen of Collections! This achievement still hangs on my office wall today.

These are the special moments we cherish as leaders, the personal and group victories of our excellent employees. They are also the times that team members will never forget. Everyone loves to be a winner. Celebrating each day's victories is what makes work fun.

I asked everyone on the team that day, "What was the best gift you ever received at work?" Everyone concluded the Tiffany silver necklace at their five-year anniversary. I asked what they would like after that. They replied, "Real food: pizza, sandwiches, and Mexican food." I'm planning a real food luncheon to celebrate our next team win!

Chapter 2

WORDS

Leaders need to understand how profoundly
they affect people, how their optimism and pessimism
are equally infectious, how directly they set the tone
and spirit of everyone around them.
                                    –Captain D. Michael Abrashoff

A leader's job is to unleash their team's full potential. Given the right circumstances, there are few limits to what can be achieved. On a high-functioning team, people need to feel a sense of belonging, self-esteem, and idealism. Achieving your vision together requires motivation and inspiration. This will require appealing to individual human needs, values, goals, and dreams.

Needed change requires leadership. You are addressing issues and putting them out in the open in order to find solutions. Hopefully, you are fighting problems to be solved together, and not fighting each other. Uniting and aligning your team toward a common goal is influenced by the words of the leader.

Twenty Motivational Phrases for Leaders

We can do it!

–Rosie the Riveter

In a famous World War II poster, Rosie the Riveter gives out the battle cry, "We can do it!" Or, as a plaque on President Ronald Reagan's Oval Office desk read, "It can be done." If you want to increase motivation, start with these words of encouragement. Here are twenty additional motivational phrases that you can use:

1. *Great to have you with us.*
2. *You're amazing!*
3. *I believe in you.*
4. *You're a star!*
5. *It's a joy to work with you.*
6. *Thank you for all that you contribute to our team.*
7. *Great job!*
8. *You make us smile.*
9. *I love your positive attitude!*
10. *Today is going to be fun!*
11. *You're special.*
12. *We're so proud of you.*
13. *You're incredible!*
14. *You make our day!*
15. *Thank you for your thoughtfulness.*
16. *We appreciate you.*
17. *Great to have you on our team.*
18. *High five!*
19. *You ROCK!*
20. *Well done!*

Recognize publicly the value of each person's work. Emphasize that you appreciate each member's contributions.

Help each employee to grow professionally and have high self-esteem. Highlight each person's accomplishments and let them know that everyone in the office notices their work, appreciates it, and cares about them.

No matter what your position, or where you fall on your organization's chart, each of us can lead through the work that we do. The more leadership opportunities that you share with your team members, the more an individual entrepreneurial attitude will take hold.

CONFLICTING LEADERSHIP

When conflicts arise among roles, such as between practice owner and practice manager for example, resort back to your shared vision, and to your core values. Remember your mission. Ours is "Caring Professionals Serving Valued Patients." This sentiment links everyone together and signals that we are collaborative rather than competitive. Keep communicating openly to get back on track and remind everyone that they are there to work together.

Conflicting leadership may also occur between front office and back clinical teams or between staff members. When this occurs, try cross-training front office and back office. Continue to build trust and understanding with a team social outing. If informal networks do not exist among your team, create them. This is a major step toward having an aligned team.

SIX KEY ATTRIBUTES OF A PROFESSIONAL

> *Professional is not a label you give yourself—*
> *it's a description you hope others will apply to you.*
> –David Maister

Strictly speaking, a professional is one who takes an oath to put others before themselves. Professionalism is, at its core, about service. Professionalism is not the job you do; it's how you do your job. We want our leaders and team members in dentistry to be professional. Part of your task as owner and leader of your dental office is to coach your team to establish and maintain professional standards. Let's look at six key attributes of a professional as a place to start:

1. *Ethical*
2. *Emotionally intelligent*
3. *Competent*
4. *Accountable*
5. *Knowledgeable*
6. *Poised*

Ethical is top of the list for professionalism. When I think of the two best professional orthodontic leaders I have ever known, they were both inclusive and respectful of all members, spending time to develop other leaders who went on to serve the orthodontic profession. They were model professionals.

Should you accept a leadership position in your office or professional society, be aware that you will not be able to control how others respond or act. You are there to serve and set a good example. Some may try to demean your efforts. Don't get discouraged. Tell others why you are pursuing your aims for the organization. Help them see how they can benefit from these goals too, and how the group can benefit from the changes that you are proposing. Do not focus on the non-supporters. Gather your mentors and support network to energize yourself to stay strong as a leader.

THE AMERICAN DENTAL ASSOCIATION CODE OF ETHICS

A man without ethics is a wild beast loosed upon this world.
–Albert Camus

By definition, ethical leaders abide by a code of ethics. They are in service, not benefitting themselves or feeding their own ego by being a "leader." We expect our dental leaders to be ethical. Let's review ethics by taking a look at the American Dental Associations' Code of Ethics.

1. *Self-governance—"Democratic leadership"*
2. *Nonmaleficence—"Do no harm"*

3. *Beneficence*—*"Do good"*
4. *Justice*—*"Fairness"*
5. *Veracity*—*"Truthfulness"*

Let's look closer at these broad categories of ethics as they apply to leadership and teamwork in dentistry.

1. SELF-GOVERNANCE—DEMOCRATIC LEADERSHIP

Citizens of democratic governments—Netherlands, Denmark, Switzerland, New Zealand, and the United States—are, in general, also the happiest. When free elections are undertaken, and everyone believes that the results are legitimate, the happiness of the citizens rises.

Similarly, whether in a volunteer dental society or in the dental office, participation and the feeling that one has control over the work that they do leads to enjoyment. The dental team and dentist want to have their voices heard. Even in a dental society, with a nomination committee that chooses the recommendations for appointment to office, there is still the possibility that a candidate can be nominated from the floor, or as a self-nomination, and win by majority vote in a democratic, self-governance forum.

2. DO NO HARM—NONMALEFICENCE

"Primum non nocere" means "First, do not harm" to patients. But we can also do harm to team members and colleagues within an organization without a code of ethics. One sure way to do so is via gossip, which can destroy office and organizational culture as well as do harm to an individual. If a gossiper has an issue with someone, they should talk directly to that person to improve the situation. Gossip is rarely positive.

When gossip is untrue, it is slander. Now you have an ethical dilemma. If left unhandled, you have a hostile environment. The gossiper must be addressed. If you are the leader, it is your obligation to put an end to such unethical behavior.

Don't think that dental professionals don't gossip and slander each other. I assure you they do. This is perhaps dentistry's worst downfall. Put another way, this is bullying. ***Bullying cannot be tolerated in the dental*** *profession.* Bullying is a symptom of laissez-faire leadership—in other words, no leadership at all.

3. *Do Good—Beneficence*

Dentists must treat their patients and staff well and also maintain kind professional relationships with their colleagues. If you are a dentist, you are not only a leader in your office but also in your community. Dentists must conduct themselves in a professional manner. As a dentist, you not only represent yourself and your office, but also the profession of dentistry.

In the workplace, dentists have the obligation to provide respectful and collaborative relationships for all those involved in oral health care.

4. *Be Fair—Justice*

Professionals have a duty to be fair in their dealings with patients, colleagues, and society. In terms of leadership, this applies to members of your professional society. Here, all are to be included without prejudice or discrimination while being given *equal opportunity to participate and serve.*

5. *Be Truthful—Veracity*

A dentist has the obligation to be honest and trustworthy in their dealings with people. There are no secrets. This is especially true in the running of a professional society. It is also true in your dental office.

In a culture of transparency, it is the leader's obligation to give straight talk about situations in the organization. Tell the truth. Get used to saying, "I declare a breakdown!"

Here, disclosure of conflict of interest is also appropriate. Should a dentist have a monetary or special interest with a company or product promoted or endorsed by the presentation or organization, such conflict needs to be disclosed in any promotional materials and in the presentation itself. Subjective statements about the quality of dental services can also raise ethical concerns. Superlatives such as "the best," "highest quality," or "expert" may not be proven and should therefore not be used.

Eliminate Punishment

Power is of two kinds.
One is obtained by the fear of punishment
and the other by acts of love.
Power based on love is a thousand times more effective
and permanent than the one derived from fear of punishment.
                                    –Mahatma Gandhi

It is commendable to take initiative, to try something new, to go beyond the ordinary in pursuit of excellence. Only positive actions empower and motivate people to move in a positive direction. For me, to have the word "punishment" in the office Employee Handbook or in the Bylaws of a prestigious dental organization without any reference to ethics is contrary to acceptable practice. It reduces an organization to that of a fraternity house during hazing week.

Punishments are knee-jerk reactions coming from an organizational silo. These will only lead to bitterness. This person thinks, "OK, I tried to go above and beyond, but I'm the one who gets punished for it! I'll never do that again! I quit!" With punishment, you will have someone much worse than a disempowered person, you'll have a disengaged, resentful one.

If left unchecked, punishment creates a toxic environment for the entire dental organization. This is laissez-faire leadership. Disgruntled members vent to others on the team who spread the story of organizational slight.

I will never forget a "punishment" issued by an orthodontic society committee director for delay in presenting my cases to the membership. An extra presentation case was issued for all on this list, including me. That year, everyone quit this volunteer society affiliate process except me. What made matters even worse was that the punishment was issued one month after my mother died of terminal cancer. Then the mandatory scheduling of my punishment case was one week before my wedding. The person who issued the punishment verbally accosted me the day of my presentation and called me at my home on a Friday night at 8:30 p.m. Being the first woman in this society, I was afraid to speak up. But not now! Let's put an end to this cruel and unusual behavior forever. All dental societies need ethics oversight.

Get everyone in your group to foster kindness and empathy with connection. Learn from mistakes. Unconstructive rivalries may spring up between different dental silos. It could be "doctor" versus "staff," "my study club" versus "your study club," "my school" versus "your school," or "my family dental legacy" versus "you the outsider." Such entrenched ways of thinking and interacting could result in an "either my way or the highway" ultimatum that devolves into people quitting. Resentments fracture the team as do unearned entitlements and unfairness.

For this reason, it is vital for your dental organization to have a code of ethics spelled out in the Team Handbook or Policies and Procedures Manual. Core values such as clinical excellence, scientific inquiry, and service to the profession remind colleagues why they have come together. Dental organizations today need leadership more than ever. That means fairness to all members, equity, and inclusion if our dental societies are to survive into the future.

LEARN TO SAY "NO"

> *If it is not right, do not do it; if it is not true, do not say it.*
> –Marcus Aurelius

When you start your position of leadership, you will be tested. Those within your organization may even give you a ridiculous request to see how you will react. One of the first acts of leadership, day one, is the ability to take charge of the situation by saying, "No."

No is actually a powerful, useful, and *positive* word when it comes to establishing your leadership. This is especially true for women leaders. You may even be heckled. Learn to say, "This is not right." Learn to say, "No."

The lack of the ability to say "No" can cause leadership to start out poorly. When leaders don't say "No" to undesirable behavior, they are saying "Yes" to trouble. They are in effect giving in to laissez-fair leadership. This is when the bullying starts, whether it is within a dental office or within a professional dental association.

Effective leaders have the discipline to say, for example, "No, you will not be getting a raise by threatening to quit." In this not uncommon office scenario, be prepared by having in place a raise process which takes into consideration the collections of the office and the annual review process. Otherwise, team members will constantly threaten to leave, telling you that there is a higher-paying job elsewhere. There is always a higher-paying job elsewhere. I have said in the past, "Don't tell me you can get $2 an hour more somewhere else, and I won't tell you that I can get someone for $2 less."

In January 2023, the state of California is issuing a mandatory $22/hr. salary for all food workers. How is this going to affect entry level dental assistants? Are young dental assistants still in training going to leave dentistry to go work for $22/hr. at McDonald's? This will be a time when the value and benefits of working in the rewarding and fulfilling atmosphere of a dental office are really going to need to be expressed and emphasized. What will give you peace of mind is being proactively prepared with HR conversations that you can deliver with courage, reminding team members why they will benefit from staying in dentistry.

INTEGRITY

> *Have the courage to say no.*
> *Have the courage to face the truth.*
> *Do the right thing because it is right.*
> *These are the magic keys to living your life with integrity.*
> –W. Clement Stone

Warren Buffet said that in looking for people to hire, he looks for three qualities: integrity, intelligence, and energy. Visionary business leaders also start with integrity, that unwavering adherence to principles on which mutual trust can be based. This is perhaps their top trait in their attitude toward life. One of the most important ways to manifest integrity is to be loyal to those who are not present.

In your professional dental career, you will face requests, challenges, and situations when you need to make the decision to adhere to your own code of ethics, staying in sync with truth, justice, and fairness. You are the maintainer of your own integrity. Guard it and protect it by doing what is right, not what is easy.

CASE STUDY 1: THE UNEMPLOYMENT COMPENSATION ABUSER

Alice read the email from her society colleague:

> *I need to officially identify you as person and business owner whom I actively asked for a job. Unless I hear from you, I will add you to work-search records.*

This dentist had sold his practice and retired several years earlier. He rarely attended meetings and his status was listed as "retired." Another member from the society had asked him to work one day a week in his office. Recently, offices were closed due to COVID-19. Significantly, during the pandemic, state unemployment compensation rules were loosed to allow self-employed individuals, such as locum tenens, to receive unemployment compensation.

Alice knew this person never actively asked for a job, sent a resume, or called her office. She had no job posting. She never received a letter, resume, phone call, or even an email from this person inquiring about employment. In addition, this person lived two and a half hours away from her practice. This email exchange followed:

Alice: "What is this?"

Colleague: "It is a form from the Unemployment Benefits Department asking for work search information for me to continue to get my unemployment payments. In the past, all I needed to do was to apply."

Alice: "No. Definitely not! Do not list me. The last thing in the world I want is any problem with the Unemployment Benefits Department!"

Colleague: "Some help you are."

His next email read: "Never mind, I found a friend who allowed me to list him."

Solution:

The most powerful word in Marketing is, "Yes." Often, the most powerful word in leadership is, "No." Always tell the truth. Do what is right. Transparency builds integrity. Without integrity, it is difficult to succeed in business or in life.

TAKE A STAND

As a leader, you're the only one who can overcome the obstacles in your practice or in your society. It's all on you. This is especially true when you are presented with an unconscionable violation of integrity. Realize that when addressing the most daunting problems, you have the power to choose how to react. You always have control over your actions.

There are many threats to integrity that you will face when running your dental practice. Examples include cheating on reported hours worked, embezzlement, lying, stealing, and the list goes on. Do not be paralyzed by the fear that you may unsettle someone by addressing the unacceptable behavior. This untrustworthy employee needs to go. It is unprofessional and a lack of leadership to not speak up. Take a stand. Sometimes you simply need to be Dr. No.

If you see that something or someone is derailing your organization, being silent is not a good decision. Similarly, the act of speaking behind a colleague's back about poor performance rather than speaking to them directly is unacceptable. Tackle problems head-on.

Your goal is to **always act with integrity.** Failing to speak up is an abdication of leadership responsibility. Take up the mantle of leadership to protect your business and elevate your team.

UBUNTU

> *I am because we are.*
> —Ubuntu African proverb

The African philosophy of *ubuntu* has as a guiding principle that "We are all in it together." This is a feeling of "humanity toward others." Nelson

Mandela practiced ubuntu when he invited his jailors to his inauguration as honored guests.

Some Bantu tribes take wrongdoers to the center of the village and surround them with tribespeople, who speak only of the good the person has done. The ritual encourages the wrongdoer to reconnect with their better self and their good behavior. Unity, harmony, and compassion are believed to help change bad behavior more than punishment ever could. The ritual of ubuntu is uplifting for the participants too—it's a win-win.

Case Study 2: Ubuntu

Allison had survived more than two decades in a toxic organizational culture. Instead of co-elevation and meritocracy, this guiding principle was "let's see how we can put others down." She vowed that if she were ever in a leadership position, these negative attitudes would be changed for the better and inappropriate comments would end.

When she became program chair, Allison did the unthinkable. She placed the prototypical unsupportive person first on the speaker program. She personally invited this toxic offender to take center stage. He responded favorably, rising to the occasion.

His behavior improved. Relationships improved. It was an ubuntu win for group dynamics!

Solution:

When possible, put the most troublesome person in the spotlight.

I remember having a troublesome team member. She was always complaining. Her attitude was negative. She was unpleasant. But she was a fantastic dental assistant in her technical skills and had many other good qualities.

At the annual team advance (not a retreat!), I put her in charge of the attitude test for the entire office. In the back of Jeffrey Gitomer's *Little Gold Book of YES! Attitude,* you can find this test, which highlights many actions that contribute to a negative work environment. By bringing awareness to harmful behaviors, a person can work to eliminate them to become a pleasant team member with whom others enjoy working.

Our entire team took the attitude test under Miss Negativity's leadership. Guess what? It worked! Her negative attitude improved. Everyone's attitude improved. Try it yourself. You will be thrilled with the results!

Chapter 3

CLARITY

Clarity precedes success.

–Robin Sharma

When building clarity in your organization, you need to repeat over and over again core values, mission, standards of professional behavior, policies and procedures, and local, state, and federal employment laws. You need to be clear about what might seem like mundane matters in order to ensure that there is no misunderstanding and that applicable statutes are being followed.

There must be clarity about what organizational excellence looks like. Don't be caught saying, "That's not what I wanted!" There must be a shared understanding and acceptance of policies in order for your office or organization to run smoothly.

THREE INTERVIEW QUESTIONS

*What makes "Hungry, Humble, and Smart" powerful and unique is
not the individual attributes themselves,
but rather the required combination of all three.*
–Patrick Lencioni

During the interview process, you are given a short time to assess the character of your potential hire. You want your interviewee to be hungry, humble, and smart. These are the three key virtues of the ideal team player outlined by teamwork author Patrick Lencioni in his book, *The Ideal Team Player: How to Recognize and Cultivate the Three Essential Virtues.* Here are three interview questions that you can ask to assess character, either during an employment interview or an intra-office review:

1. WHAT IS THE HARDEST THAT YOU'VE EVER WORKED ON SOMETHING IN YOUR LIFE?

Hungry people almost never have to be pushed. They are self-motivated. They work hard. They are able to sustain commitment to doing a job well. They pursue excellence in all that they do.

2. TELL US ABOUT SOMEONE WHO IS BETTER THAN YOU IN AN AREA THAT REALLY MATTERS TO YOU.

Humility is perhaps the number-one virtue of an ideal team player. A humble person will emphasize team over self. They will share credit and not be arrogant or self-centered. Humility is not a lack of self-confidence. It isn't thinking less of yourself; humility is thinking of yourself less.

3. WHAT DO YOU DO THAT PEOPLE IN YOUR PERSONAL LIFE MIGHT FIND ANNOYING?

No one is perfect. Emotional intelligence includes knowing your personal weaknesses and working on them. In this regard, being smart refers to common sense and awareness. Smart people have good judgement and understand group dynamics.

You can review these questions with your employees at your team meeting and share your answers with each other. This can be a valuable self-awareness exercise. Discuss with your team why these three virtues are a requirement for a job in your office.

At the end of the book *The Ideal Team Player,* there is an employee self-assessment exercise. It is a fantastic self-improvement, ownership, and development practicum for the entire office. Take this test together and discuss the results.

The Team Handbook

> *Working in an office without a team handbook*
> *is like living in a lawless land.*
> –Ann Marie Gorczyca

Imagine it's the first day of employment and the person conducting the onboarding says:

> "Welcome. Please take an hour to read the Team Handbook. Do you have any questions? Please sign the Acknowledgement Form indicating that you understand what is written here and what is expected of you as a member of our excellent team. Welcome to the team! We believe in you and we welcome your participation. Glad you're here."

In documenting how things run in your office or organization, no detail is too small. If you want to build clarity of communication with your team, then start with the Team Handbook, your basic Policies and Procedures Manual for your dental office. Everything important to employment must be included there. If you want to build clarity in your dental society, start with the Policies and Procedures and the Bylaws. Policies and Procedures Manuals and Bylaws are also basically your organization Team Handbooks.

It is said that CEOs of major corporations always have these foundational documents readily available. If someone were to take over your office or society today, would they be able to figure out how your organization runs by what is documented in your written guidelines? If you seek a miscommunication-free life, start there.

Teams have rules. The Team Handbook should clearly outline expected behavior. As an organization evolves, the Handbook is continuously updated to reflect the way things are, including current employment laws. By knowing the rules, problems and misunderstandings are minimized.

It's said that the Ritz Carlton customer service handbook, commonly referred to as "MR. BIV" (standing for Mistakes, Reworks, Breakdowns, Inefficiencies, and Variations), has over one thousand entries and is continuously updated. Take time to document what goes wrong in your office, correct these mistakes, and include the positive changes in your Handbook so that your systems are continuously improving.

Employment law attorney Peter Finn of the firm Bradley, Curley, Barrabee & Kowalski, P.C., Larkspur, California, recommends that certain details **not** be written in the employee Team Handbook. For example, he recommends **not** having a corrective action policy written in your Team Handbook manual because it could create an expectation that certain procedures must be followed before termination. This may become troublesome in an emergency termination situation.

POLICIES AND PROCEDURES

In a nonprofit organization, the Policies and Procedures Manual documents the roles of officers, the duties of committees, and expected processes. Policies and Procedures should always be followed and updated. The Policies and Procedures Manual in essence is the Team Handbook of your dental society. If these guidelines are not being followed, why do you have them?

Your Policies and Procedures Manual is a living document. Your dental organization will continue to run based upon these clearly outlined and codified expectations.

Case Study 3: Ten Years of Vacation

Sally worked for her local dental society as executive director for ten years. When the new president checked her vacation hours accrued, he discovered that this software program had never been activated! This had been Sally's job to do but she had never done it!

The organization had been paying for this HR software for ten years, yet no one had taken the time to enter the vacation accrual information into the computer or verify that it was ever done. Now the dental society had to "take Sally's word" and pay Sally for ten years of "unused" paid vacation!

Solution:

Be careful to always document and maintain awarded and accrued paid vacation hours in your payroll software. Maintain a copy in each employee file. Update this tally each time the team member takes a vacation. Review the unused vacation time at each individual employee annual review to ensure that their vacation data has been recorded properly. Your state may not have a "use it or lose it" vacation law policy. For more information for California vacation pay law, visit https://www.dir.ca.gov/dise/fag_vacation.htm. Readers are encouraged to check employment laws in their own state and consult an HR attorney.

Policy Acceptance

It is critical that the values are clearly
understood by everyone.

–Horst Schulze

When there is a misunderstanding of a policy, you should be able to refer to the Team Handbook as a document of clarity and fairness that describes expectations of your staff and the accepted terms of their employment. If you are president of a society, there is no one there to teach you what to do when you start your leadership position. There is no lesson in how to verify that all the important tasks of the organization are being done. You learn as you go.

As a new leader, you might not know what the tasks of the society are or the committees or board members. First, read the most recent Policies and Procedures Manual as a guide. As your board members or others may also be new, distribute a copy of the documents to everyone involved. This is where mutual understanding and working together as a team begins.

Case Study 4: The No-Surprise Retainer Bill

Susie was excited to be working in an orthodontic office. She had wanted to do so for years. She had five children who all needed braces and she needed braces herself. She knew that the office provided the employment benefit of orthodontic services at no charge for children of employees as well as the employee herself.

There was just one expense. As written in the Team Handbook, when employees receive free orthodontic services as a benefit, the employee must pay for their own lab bill. Whether this bill is for retainers or Invisalign, the employee must pay the bill in full, within thirty days of receipt.

Susie was also a career climber. Once all five of her children's braces and her braces were off—almost all finishing in the same month—she moved on to her new job for one dollar per hour more. Before leaving her present position, she was given the lab bill for six sets of retainers.

Susie claimed she didn't know she would be responsible for the retainer bill. She demanded that the office pay her bill.

Solution:

Unless you plan to pay all lab bills for free treatment done in your office for employees and their dependents, be sure to **have a written office policy in the Team Handbook that all lab bills for free employment benefit dental services be paid by the employee.** Provided that you have retained a signed signature of acceptance of this office policy, simply send the employee the bill for their lab services. You could also ask the lab owner, who may also know the employee, to give the bill directly to the employee and not list these services on the office lab bill.

Your Team Handbook is not only your employer-employee work agreement outlining the rules of the office but also the employee benefits document of your office. Just as patients need to sign various forms (medical history, term and conditions of service, diagnosis and treatment plans, and financial contract), your employees must also sign a form confirming that they have read and understand the Team Handbook as the accepted terms of their employment.

EMPLOYMENT LAW

> *No man is above the law,*
> *and no man is below it.*
> –Theodore Roosevelt

Human resource management is half psychology, half employment law. No one is above the law. If you own a business and have employees, you've got plenty of employment laws to follow.

In my book, *Beyond the Morning Huddle: Human Resource Management for a Successful Dental Office*, I list employment laws and discuss how they affect dental practices. As a small business owner, it is imperative that you are up-to-date with employment laws. They are ever-present and there can be serious repercussions in cases of non-adherence.

Your team members must follow local, state, and federal employment laws. Breaking the law is not an option. You can't keep an employee who does not follow the law. Doing otherwise is a liability for any business owner and a risk not worth taking.

I always tell my team, "If you want to break the law and drive ninety miles an hour on the highway, you will get a speeding ticket and that will cost you a lot of money. If **you** break the law in my dental office, **I** will have to pay the consequences. I'm not willing to do that." Let's avoid costly HR land mines.

Having a Team Handbook and closely reviewing and following employment laws are critical for building an office climate of trust. Team members will ask, "Is this a trustworthy, law-abiding office?" Start times, stop times, vacation-day requests, and sick days need to be reported honestly and transparently, with no surprises.

Enforcing Employment Laws

> *It is time to restore the American precept that*
> *each individual is accountable for his actions.*
> –Ronald Reagan

It is the duty of the practice owner to review applicable employment laws with the team, document necessary law-abiding information in the Team Handbook, and enforce local, state, and federal employment laws. Staff actions will sometimes present challenges to employment laws. In California, we need to take a mandatory two-hour employment law course every two years as a requirement for licensure.

The HR coordinator who calls in payroll also has the important duty to understand employment laws. She can have each employee sign their time sheet verifying that the hours listed are accurate and that they have taken their breaks. *This documents that the team member has taken their ten-minute breaks and thirty-minute lunches as specified by California state law.*

The US Department of Labor does consider breaks as compensable work hours. Check the break laws in your state at https://www.dol.gov/agencies/whd/state.meal-breaks. Confirm that you and your team are compliant with state break laws.

The Nonexempt Employee

Nowhere is following employment law more critical than in California, implementing the minimum thirty-minute lunch break for a nonexempt employee. A nonexempt employee is paid by the hour. Unless you are the office manager, making hiring decisions, and earning over $55,000 per year, most team members in dentistry are nonexempt employees. *Nonexempt employees must take a lunch break for a minimum of a half-hour after four hours and fifty-nine minutes in the state of*

California if they work an eight-hour day. Even if you have a "lunch and learn" presentation provided by a company representative, the employee still must sign out for their half-hour lunch break. ***The employee must be completely free during his/her lunch.*** The employee can agree to waive this meal period provided that they do not work more than six hours in the work day.

There is no such thing as "voluntary" in employment law. Should the employee and doctor/owner not follow employment law, they open themselves up to future scrutiny from the local, state, and federal Departments of Labor (DOL) and taxation bureaus.

Lunches are built into the office schedule. Lunch in our office is one and a half hours long. This gives me time to have lunch with a referring doctor and gives every employee time to go home for lunch if they wish. The two receptionists share the lunch break, each taking forty-five minutes, so that the phone can still be answered during the break time.

On nondoctor days, a nonexempt employee has two choices: Work for five hours fifty-nine minutes straight, and then be done for the day, or work no more than four hours and fifty-nine minutes, clock out for a minimum of a half-hour lunch, and return to complete an eight-hour day. These are the only two employment options in the state of California without penalty. http://wwwdir.cagov/dlse/faq_mealperiods.htm.

CASE STUDY 5: WORKING SEVEN HOURS STRAIGHT IN CALIFORNIA

On Mondays, Cindy normally works a six straight, clocking out after five hours and fifty-nine minutes, without lunch. The doctor arrives fifteen minutes before the end of her day and asks her to stay to finish some additional tasks. Cindy stays past the 5:59. She works seven hours straight, without a lunch break. Cindy earns thirty dollars per hour in regular pay. How much do you owe Cindy for her prolonged work day in the state of California?

Solution:

Because Cindy missed her lunch, an employer in the state of California must pay one additional *penalty hour*. You must pay her for the seven hours that she worked plus the one-hour penalty pay for the missed lunch break. You owe Cindy $240.

Case Study 6: Not Taking a Thirty-Minute Lunch Break in California

Nicole only took a twenty-minute lunch break and then clocked back in. She then worked an 8.66-hour day. What must you pay Nicole in the state of California?

Solution:

Nicole was asked why she did not take her full lunch break. She answered that she finished her lunch quickly and wanted to return to work to be with her friends. Provide documented counseling and tell Nicole that you did not request that she return to work early. Have her write her excuse on the time sheet and have her sign it. **Give Nicole the one hour of penalty premium pay for not taking her half-hour lunch break.** Document that she was told that her conduct violated office policy and, if repeated, could lead to discipline.

She would receive the normal eight hours of pay that she worked with .66 hours of overtime pay plus one hour of pay penalty. The premium pay penalty is not included in the overtime calculation.

Case Study 7: Four Ten-Hour Days

You and your team must decide that you would like to adopt the 4/10 work week. You have a unanimous vote that everyone accepts the ten-hour work day. Your Team Handbook is revised to reflect that the forty-hour work week is now four ten-hour days. You and your team, however, clock on average, eight and one-half hours each day. What do you do?

Solution:

You must pay for the ten-hour day. You cannot adopt a 4/10 work week to avoid overtime. You must pay for the four ten-hour days if that is to be the established work schedule. You cannot send employees home early with less than ten hours of pay after adopting the 4/10 work schedule.

There are very strict procedural requirements that must be followed in order to lawfully implement a 4/10 workweek, or other alternative workweek schedules. This includes registering with the state's online database. In California, go to https://www.dir.ca.gov/databases/oprl/dlsr-awe.html.

The Occupational Safety and Health Administration explains that longer working hours can lead to worker fatigue, increased levels of stress, poor eating habits, lack of physical activity, and illness. Personally, I prefer to have an eight-hour work day, a four-day work week, and pay overtime.

THE EXEMPT EMPLOYEE

The Fair Labor Standards Act (FLSA) rules for exempt versus nonexempt job status are specific. In order to classify as exempt from federal overtime rules, the employee must pass three tests:

1. They must be paid a minimum of $455 per week.
2. They must have a fixed salary. Any day that the exempt employee works, they must be paid their full salary.
3. The employee must meet the duties of an administrator, executive, or professional.

Exempt versus nonexempt status and overtime are often at the center of many DOL and tax bureau audits. *Do a self-audit of your exempt status and nonexempt employees' overtime and document your efforts.* Make this part of your HR review process. (These rules vary from state to state.)

OVERTIME

Overtime, when accumulated, must always be paid. From the viewpoint of optimal practice management, what constitutes excessive overtime? For a full-time employee working fifty weeks per year and thirty-six to forty hours per week, fifty hours or less per year is acceptable overtime. If overtime is more than that, examine the work schedule to discover where, when, and why you are running into overtime problems.

Include a provision in your Team Handbook that overtime must be preapproved. Scheduling a seven and one-half hour work day may minimize overtime.

Nonexempt Bonus Law and Calculations

As your aim is fostering teamwork, when goals are achieved and it's time to celebrate, the bonus goes to the entire team, including the doctor. It takes a village to meet or exceed practice goals, so all should share in the reward.

Set a goal for bonuses that applies to everyone. As an employer, you want to reward teamwork, perseverance, and a job well done. You should reward the team for reaching the goal, optionally with a monetary bonus.

Well, not so fast! You want to give everyone the same amount. But wait! The employee with overtime must receive more! ***Employers must pay overtime on nondiscretionary bonuses!*** FLSA requires that the amount of the incentive be included in the employee's "regular rate" for the purpose of calculating overtime. The FLSA divides bonuses into two categories: discretionary and nondiscretionary.

A discretionary bonus must meet the following criteria:

1. Employer retains discretion as to payment.
2. Employer retains discretion as to the amount.
3. Employer retains discretion until near the end of the period which it covers.
4. The bonus must not be paid pursuant to any prior contract, agreement, or promise.

Nondiscretionary bonuses are promised bonuses and are given for a certain reason, which was agreed upon with the team. Once stated, it is, therefore, a contractual bonus. These are the most common reasons for nondiscretionary bonuses:

- Productivity (group or individual)
- Quality of work
- Attendance

- Length of service
- Safety

If an employee expects the bonus based on achieved performance, that bonus is considered to be nondiscretionary. There are two ways in which nondiscretionary bonuses can be paid.

Two Nondiscretionary Bonus Options

1. Flat Rate Percentage Bonus

The employee worked eighty-two hours the last two weeks of the month.

80 hours x $20 (regular rate) = $1,600

2 hours overtime x $20 (1.5 x $20 x 2) = $60

Gross earnings to the employee are $1,660. Bonus is 12% of gross earnings: $1,660 x 12% = $199.20

Total two-week earnings = $1,859.20

In this example, no additional calculation is required for purposes of determining overtime. Everyone would receive the same percentage regardless of their payrate. Therefore, bonuses would not be equal.

2. Overtime Plus Premium Bonus

If the bonus is earned over a period of time (a month, for example), it becomes a little more complicated. You would prorate the bonus equally over the period it was earned and make the overtime calculation based on the amount.

A $200 bonus is given to everyone for one month's production. Nonexempt employees with no overtime would be given the addition of a $200 bonus on their end-of-month paycheck. A nonexempt employee with overtime would receive the $200 bonus plus premium overtime cal-culated as follows:

The employee worked 160 hours for the month plus two hours of overtime in the last two weeks.

The employee's hourly rate including overtime now becomes:

160 hours for the month x $20 hour = $3,200 for the month

$3,200 + $200 = $3,400 / 160 hours = $21.25/hour

Overtime must be paid in the new hourly rate.

2 hours overtime x $21.25 (1.5 x $21.25) = $31.875

Gross earnings to the employee are now:

80 hours x $20 (regular rate) = $1,600

$200 bonus = $1,800

2 hours premium overtime x $21.25 (1.5 x $21.25 x 2) = $63.75

Total two-week earnings = $1,863.75

In this example, the bonus is prorated over the time it was earned, and the overtime bonus is based on that amount.

For more information on nondiscretionary bonuses, see https://www.dol.gov.agencies/whd/fact-sheets/56c-bonuses and https://www.dir.ca.gov/dise/fag_overtime.htm#~:text=Yes%2C%20if%20it%20is%20a,bonuses%20include%20flat%20sum%20bonuses.

Abiding Laws, Policies and Procedures, and Bylaws

If you need assistance in the area of employment law, have a low threshold to consult an HR professional or an attorney. Issue a notice to document what your team needs to understand so that applicable laws and policies and procedures can be appropriately followed.

A dental society not following Policies and Procedures, Bylaws, or Nonprofit Governance laws becomes more problematic since they are a volunteer organization. Make sure that you have Nonprofit Directors & Officers insurance for all board members so that no one is personally liable should an undesirable situation arise. The Annual Report to Members should disclose financial status. Maintain careful records in case you are audited.

A Three-Year Payroll Audit

Some dental attorneys are now recommending a three-year employment audit to new buyers of dental practices. Whether you are a seller or a buyer of a dental practice, making up for not following compensation employment laws is something no one wants to deal with. The last thing you want is to have to make up for unpaid overtime during retirement.

Payouts of monies due to employees under the law may also include penalties. It is better to follow explicitly every aspect of employment law. Dentists can be personally liable for nonpayment of wages, even if they are incorporated.

Disclaimer: I am not an attorney and am not providing legal advice. I am merely an orthodontist, employer, and author trying to study and disseminate with my colleagues the importance of employment law knowledge in the running of your dental practice. When it comes to issues of employment, readers are advised to consult an HR attorney.

Chapter 4

CANDOR

You can't build a reputation on what you are going to do.
                                                      –Henry Ford

A leader speaks candidly. When speaking about performance, remember that the numbers set you free. This is why reports are important. When considering reports, ask, "How could these numbers be improved?"

TRUTH

Look reality straight in the eye
and then act upon it with as much speed as you can.
                                                      –Jack Welch

If the ship goes down in dentistry, the storm is usually about not having enough money. Revenue comes in the form of new patients. Be frank about cash flow. Numbers are the language of business.

This is why I love open-book management. The business owner does not carry the financial burden alone nor is it a burden at all. The bottom line is the score of everyone on the team who contributed to it by their level of action. The leader steers based on the results of the team and makes decisions based upon performance metrics.

Raises are dependent on increased cash flow. With an open-book approach, all can see the team's performance. There is no greater motivation for team accountability than review of the data. You're all in it together. In this way, keeping score can even be exciting and fun.

FIFTEEN BARRIERS TO TRUTH TELLING

How many times has a team member quit employment and, after their departure, you find that some tasks have not been done? Perhaps there is some issue that needs resolution that the departing team member never told you about. At some point, the issue becomes overwhelming to them and rather than confiding in the doctor and the team, the employee prefers to quit.

We have a mantra in our office: "Only the truth shall be spoken." Coach K in his book *Teamwork* shares this tenet: "Whether it's good or bad, only the truth shall be spoken. And, I want to hear it right away."

This is easier said than done, asking for only the truth and getting it. In his book *Leading the Unleadable: How to Manage Mavericks, Cynics, Divas, and Other Difficult People*, author Alan Willett, president of Oxseeker, an organization of culture-change consultancy, states that there are fifteen reasons employees may not tell the truth:

1. *Fear of disappointing the boss.*
2. *Self-doubt.*
3. *Fear of career repercussions.*
4. *Fear of losing customers.*
5. *Fear of conflict.*
6. *Denial.*
7. *No one else thinks it is a problem.*
8. *Low self-esteem.*
9. *Fear of the issue sticking to them.*
10. *Low communication skill.*
11. *Confusion.*
12. *Thinking someone else will take care of it.*
13. *Fear that nothing will happen.*

14. Not my problem.
15. Protecting others.

The truth will set us free. Build a climate of comfort in the truth in your office. Make communicating the truth the easy, automatic action of choice.

BLIND SPOTS

> *Unless you look carefully at the facts*
> *and separate them from your assumptions,*
> *your entire strategy will lead you in the wrong direction.*
> –Thomas D. Zweifel

It is impossible for the leader to see and hear everything that goes on in the dental office. The team must have the conviction and agency to bring important issues out in the open. It is also of utmost importance that everyone on the team speaks the unvarnished truth: an honest and realistic appraisal about where the office stands today.

It does not serve the office well to be delusional or falsely optimistic. It also does not help to talk wishfully about what should be or what will be. **It only helps to talk about where we are right now and what we must do today to achieve our goals.**

There is one way to reveal a blind spot: hire a consultant and have an external assessment. I have done this in order to educate and develop myself and my entire team. Consultants can review reports and provide recommendations remotely. Consultants arc also available to train your staff on individual tasks. To find a good consultant, start with those recommended by your systems management software company. Others work with dental practice management companies.

Risk Disagreement

> *The art of communication is the language of leadership.*
> —James Humes

Every time you speak, you are auditioning for leadership. Speak with clarity and confidence and be sure to communicate every small win of the entire office. Share all concerns. This is why the group meetings are so important. It is time to give everyone the opportunity to speak. It gives you time to discuss strategy for making the office the best that it can be. The overall success of the office is reflective of each team member's individual contribution. You're all in it together. The more you can express this fact, the better.

In his book *True North: Emerging Leader Edition,* author and former CEO Bill George describes the first African American female CEO, Ursula Burns, as someone who isn't one to withhold her opinions, quoting her own words as someone who "has always been blunt." As leader, she needed this impatient communication style to steer Xerox Corporation away from impending bankruptcy. Ursula Burns did not want to be defined by diversity; she just wanted the opportunity to lead her organization. She states, "We all need to be brusquer. Risk disagreeing with each other without having to mince words. Being overly polite is such a waste of time." She stated that, at first, Xerox suffered from terminal niceness, which led to people supporting each other's mediocrity. She advises, "Don't fail to say what you truly mean."

Confidence

> *The world can't happen to you,*
> *you have to happen to the world.*
> —Ursula Burns

Studies cite women's reluctance to promote themselves in leadership. Some say that women who do promote themselves are disliked by both men and women. It's a catch-22 situation that women leaders often find themselves in.

Similarly, men love asking women for help in performing tasks. Then once help is given, if noticed by others, male leaders will reprimand a woman for helping. Here lies another catch-22 situation.

Then there are stereotypes creating ideas about how Blacks or Asians or blondes should behave, what their competence level is, and what position is suitable for them, which can be confining.

Confidence can overcome all of these situations. There is no better example of confidence than CEO Ursula M. Burns. Her no-nonsense attitude is thoroughly expressed in her memoir *Where You Are is not Who You Are,* making it one of the best leadership books I have ever read. In her own words, this she addressed in the headlines in the press, which proclaimed her as the first Black woman to lead a Fortune 500 company in this way:

"Was it truly so amazing to think a Black woman could lead a multibillion-dollar company? I had worked at Xerox for twenty-nine years starting as an intern and doing almost every job in the company. I had a strong track record. I was very well educated. I hadn't been plucked from a circus sideshow. **I earned the position.**"

Those who do the work and earn the position of leadership need and deserve to be confident. You need confidence to take the stage as leader. Front and center is a very valuable organizational space. Go forward with confidence, taking on the leadership mantle day one. Don't behave like a rookie. Whether in your office, or in your dental society, there will be others trying to impede or challenge your leadership. A loud, outspoken cynic may attempt to overtake your meeting. This could be an employee or a past president of your dental organization. Speak your truth and move on.

This is especially a problem for woman leaders. Being spoken over or being upstaged by men is common. Others may even try to monopolize conversation or take over your Zoom screen! Don't let it happen! Although difficult, deal with it. To regain control, use the statement, "Thank you very much. Let's move on." Otherwise, the cynic becomes an unofficial owner of the meeting. Embrace a leadership mindset, even when you feel that you are leading the unleadable.

CLASH

When leaders meet, whether it be in your dental office, your dental society, or even the political bodies, there will be times of destructive leadership conflict known as "clash of the titans."

As a leader, you need to "power through" all uncomfortable conversations and difficult situations. People will disagree. Some people will think that they are always right. Others will think that you are always wrong. If you want to build a strong leadership team in your dental office or society, expect some figurative "hand-to-hand combat" with titans.

Realize that titans speak up. Titans also have ideas. Titans can care. Titans will challenge you. Titans can be 100 percent dedicated. And, titans are willing to work hard.

Be fearless when dealing with titans. Be open to everyone's ideas but keep the focus on real issues and the obstacles to achieving your common goals. Constantly remind your organization of your mission statement and core values as the cornerstones of group survival and success.

SIX CRITERIA TO MAKE AN IMPROVE OR REMOVE DECISION

When I've heard all I need to make a decision,
I don't take a vote. I make a decision.
–Ronald Reagan

There will come a time when, as leader, you will face a struggle with a team member. There may be an emotional or cooperation breakdown. There could be a miscommunication. There could even be a power struggle. There might be a dysfunctional psychological illness. Don't be surprised when it happens. Expect it. Then work to prevent it from ever happening again.

At this point, a leader must ask, "Is this a performance problem?" or, "Is this a personality or emotional problem?" Performance deficiencies often cannot be fixed, even if the person is a nice person trying their best. Great HR managers know that not everyone comes with unlimited potential. It will be necessary to make a break to improve the performance of the team.

A psychological, emotional, personality, ego, or humility issue is difficult to deal with. This problem could be related to the leader, the employee, or both. It is at this time that a leader needs to realize that they cannot control other people. They can only control themselves, their own actions, and their own emotions. When a person shows up for work, but they cannot control their own mind or actions, this is something that the employee needs to fix themselves. Give them the resources to do so. The leader's job is to help the team to be successful while maintaining a safe environment.

Your leadership obligation is to the group as a whole and the success of the business or organization. If troublesome behavior is outright illegal, such as in the case of embezzlement, then making the decision to terminate an employee is extremely easy. Other situations may be more difficult. Here are six criteria which may be helpful in this decision-making process.

1. SUPPORT OF THE TEAM.

Does the individual have the support of the team? If other A+ vital team members are ready to quit unless this staff person goes, then separation is in order. This individual is fracturing the group, an impossible situation to rectify. This is why involving the whole office in the hiring process in the first place is so critical.

2. A GOOD TEAM PLAYER.

Does the individual raise the ability of the team? Pay attention to "soft skills." Collaboration shortfalls can negate positive technical skill contributions. Behavior which is undesirable, such as absenteeism, can negate any positive skills, technical or soft.

Remember, you can train almost anyone for technical proficiency. It is more difficult to change deficient soft skills such as disloyalty, selfishness, or lack of emotional intelligence. These individuals are not worth the time and treasure needed for remedial efforts, and they should not be retained.

3. *Work Toward Self-Improvement.*

Is the team member willing and do they have the ability to process the input toward their performance improvement? If the team member does not take responsibility, or always blames others for their mistakes, this is not a promising future. An effective team member must have the ability to receive and act upon feedback for improvement.

4. *An Asset, Not a Liability.*

What is the fit? Are teamwork and results better with the person present or absent? Are the individual's skills needed? As an example, since patient reminder calls are now done by electronic phone reminders and text messaging and calls can be answered offsite, are two receptionists still really needed, or do two receptionists increase social loafing and decrease efficiency? Is the person reducing team performance by causing work disruptions? Or, does the person produce poor quality work output which constantly needs to be redone?

5. *Contributions are Needed.*

Weigh current workforce size needs versus future expectation. Should it be necessary to reduce your team size, there will always be a natural attrition if you wait long enough.

Layoffs are tough on morale and need to be avoided at all costs. However, due to economic changes, increased technology, demographics, or supply-demand change, downsizing may be beneficial. Keep an eye on your current employee needs and adjust accordingly.

6. *Contributions are Vital.*

The final factor is, if this person were removed, how difficult would it be to acquire the same skills from outside the organization in a timely manner? Face it, you will need a dental assistant, receptionist, or sterilization team member, even if the current situation is ideal. It might be best to keep the team member you now have until a replacement is found, if a replacement can be found at all.

Grade these six questions from -2 to +2 to weigh your options with respect to a particular team member. As the leader, sooner or later you will be making the decision to remove or improve a team member. Sometimes it is necessary to sacrifice one to save the whole of the team, including your office, and yourself.

POOR CITIZENSHIP BEHAVIOR

No team can win without great players. *The first step in eliminating undesirable work behaviors is to clearly identify that they exist.* Next, address them. Otherwise, counterproductive work will destroy teamwork and the success of your office.

Examples of problems include absenteeism, stealing, lying, cheating, gossiping, competing, blaming, and outright bullying. Some of these behaviors may be related to deep-seated personality disorders.

If you encounter such adverse performance issues, it is your duty as the leader to courageously eliminate them as quickly as possible. You must not allow a hostile work environment to exist. Here is when the HR phrase, "Hire slow, fire fast" kicks in. It is your duty to fire fast, not only for your team and your patients, but also for yourself as leader and for the survival of your practice.

Why are dental leaders burdened by not identifying and eliminating undesirable work behaviors sooner? Are we avoiding hurting the other person's feelings or are we averse to holding an uncomfortable conversation? Are we too focused on teeth? Or, have we been in the ivory tower of dental education too long, isolated from mainstream society, to know how to effectively address its wide range of behaviors? Do we lack the courage and candor needed to take care of HR situations quickly?

To learn more about how to recognize and eliminate dysfunctional behaviors, visit my book, *Beyond the Morning Huddle: HR Management for a Successful Dental Practice.*

THREE TEAM PLAYERS TO AVOID

Most of what we learn in this crazy life is what to avoid.
–Charles Bukowski

Most leaders have some formulation for minimum requirement of a team player. I like, "Ready, willing, and able." Gino Wickman recommends, "Gets it, wants it, does it." As previously noted, Patrick Lencioni describes the ideal team player as, "Hungry, humble, and smart."

A great team member needs to exhibit all three positive performance expectations. If an employee has only two, you as the leader are in trouble. Here are three scenarios first described by Patrick Lencioni outlining that when one of the three ideals is missing, you are left with a gap in team coherence and dynamics.

1. THE SLACKER: NOT HUNGRY

The slacker has low energy or even worse, apathy. They may not get things done at all and say that work is done when it isn't. Piles of papers and work not done decorate their desk. But they're lovable and nice to be around. They smile a lot and they like you! They can even be fun. They may have a great personality and get along well with others. They're great at office parties. But they are providing companionship, not results.

You may be obliged to hire another person just to do the work done that the slacker can't get done. Perhaps they are not billing insurance. Perhaps they are not collecting accounts receivable. Attendance may also be poor as they show up late and leave early. Ultimately, their lack of performance causes problems for you and your team. Your business suffers. Their poor example of performance causes slower work from everyone and socializing overtakes your organization. Just one loveable slacker will cause an entire dental office to decline.

2. THE POLITICIAN: NOT HUMBLE

This is an all talk and no action person. The skillful politician sweet talks others. The doctor may not know that behind the scenes, this is not a team player. The politician is actually a staff splitter, who will treat those of influence well, while rank-and-file teammates may be ignored.

Organizations might not realize that the politician accomplishes nothing that moves the organization forward. The politician may end up costing the group money as they hire others to do the work which they were expected to do.

Everything is about the politician. They are not there to help their teammates. They are there to get what they can for themselves, to look good, get their picture taken, and to put yet another political office on their resume. They leave others to do the work, then they take all the credit.

The skillful politician is not afraid to make others look bad publicly. They are self-centered and selfish. They are oblivious or couldn't care less about how others feel. The people actually doing the work are forced to endure them. They have their inner circle of other politicians. They scratch each other's backs and give each other awards.

3. THE MESS MAKER: NOT SMART

A team player may be humble and they may even be hungry, but if they are not smart there will be continuous mistakes that cost you and your office valuable time and money. The messes that they make can be great, and your losses can be infinite. They could even lead you into bankruptcy. They will cause problems for you, your business, their teammates, and your patients.

Perhaps they erroneously pay payroll twice for the same period. Maybe they fail to keep up on answering phone messages. They delay paying invoices. Or, they could break expensive equipment. The accident-prone mess-maker will need continuous clean-up of their errors. It is actually easier to work without them. Even if you become short staffed and one person down in your dental office, eliminating the mess-maker will improve your teamwork, your office, and your life.

QUESTS

Without clear expectations, people are being paid to guess.
                                                                    –Henry J. Evans

The titans on your team need to be challenged to an adventurous quest. That's why, when I became the first woman president of the Northern California Angle Society of Orthodontists, I wanted to set a compelling goal to keep our team of titans focused on the future and what we could accomplish together. Our biggest challenge was to organize our first out-of-state meeting in Arizona in 2022 and our first international membership meeting in Japan in 2024.

There is excitement in quests. Make your team goal inspirational and aspirational. Think big! Working toward a goal brings a team together.

People invest in leaders who know that they are capable of the difficult journey. Members of the team will get excited about having been invited to take part. Along the way, the team will start to realize that the goal and the organization mean a lot to them. They can contribute and feel good about what they have to offer to the quest. They are part of a great team!

As leader, you may wish to give an inspirational pep talk. Great speeches have three important components:

1.   Where we have come from;
2.   Where we are now; and
3.   Where we need to go.

End your speech with what you and your team must do together to achieve your quest.

Chapter 5

ALLEGIANCE

Individual commitment to a group effort—
that's what makes a team work,
a company work, a society work, a civilization work.
–Vince Lombardi

A top priority action of the leader is to recognize, recruit, and retain talented team members. You want to ensure that all staffing that you make as leader are best for the patient, the office, and the team. In order to achieve a high level of staff allegiance, start by recruiting and recognizing "A" players. This is one of the most difficult jobs of a leader.

Remember the promise of Americans in the Pledge of Allegiance. "I pledge allegiance..." You want team members who do not want to let down their patients, their doctor, or each other. Their allegiance is also critical for their own success.

The Thirteen-Step Hiring Process

A leader needs people around her who are experts,
who know what the hell they're doing.
                                        –Ursula M. Burns

To have a great team, start by hiring "the right stuff." Time is needed to find and hire the right person for the job. Hiring is a critical decision. Take your time. Don't just hire to fill a position. Have a planned selection process. Your up-front early efforts will produce enormous back-end results in work environment satisfaction and lower team turnover. You may be spending more time with a new hire than your own spouse over the next several years. Remember the foundational HR phrase, "Hire slow, fire fast."

In my book *Beyond the Morning Huddle: HR Management for a Successful Dental Practice,* I outline a thirteen-step hiring process.

1. **Review resumes**
2. **Make initial phone calls**
3. **Check references**
4. **Office meet and greet**
5. **Conduct interview**
6. **Check current license**
7. **Skills assessment 1: working interview**
8. **Team lunch**
9. **Team meeting**
10. **Skills assessment 2: working interview**
11. **A unanimous team decision**
12. **Final background check**
13. **Job offer**

The reference check phone calls are the most important step of the hiring process. It confirms that your candidate has not been repeatedly fired.

I recently called prior employers of a new candidate who was experienced in orthodontic assisting. I asked three orthodontists with whom she had worked in the recent past the all-important question: *"**Would you rehire this person?**"*

All three responses were a resounding, "No, no, definitely not."

Without my asking, one orthodontist voluntarily added, "Let me check my HR notes. 'Does not follow chart entries, instructions, and directions. Coached employee but there was no improvement.'" Enough said. We ended up hiring a new grad and training her ourselves.

Your team plays an important part in the hiring process. In dentistry, we work closely together in a small space. The new hire must become part of the teamwork culture which has already been firmly established. It helps tremendously if the team likes and knows that they can work well with the candidate prior to onboarding. When the team fully participates in the final hiring decision, they feel as though they are "all in," with respect to making the new team member a success.

One way to achieve this objective is to have your team take the job candidate out to lunch without the doctor. In keeping with employment laws, lunch is paid as a work function; the staff is given a half-hour break after the lunch before returning back to work.

This way, your team members will get a personal feel for the candidate. Let's call it a "gut feeling." Take a poll. Do they like and want the candidate as a new team member or not?

The job applicant may behave differently when the doctor is not around. Nowhere is this truer than with "the apple polisher" candidate, one who helps the doctor but couldn't care less about the rest of the team. Ask your team members: "Is this candidate a good fit for us? Is this someone you can work with and who will be an asset to our team?" You want the answer to be an enthusiastic, "Yes!"

The candidate lunch also gives the team time to say nice things about the office without the doctor present. Your team is proud of their work, their culture, and their teamwork. Let your team promote your unique job opportunity as part of your recruitment efforts.

"I'VE GOT YOUR BACK"

These are probably the four most important words of an aligned team. They build trust and confidence. Like US Navy SEALs, a team which is devoted to the success of each other, the mission, and the leader, is unstoppable. They realize that they can count on each other for help. They're backed up, they're covered. They know that everyone on the team, including the leader, is on their side.

The oath of the team is to maintain the office culture of "I've got your back" collaboration and allegiance. It is the responsibility of an ideal team player to be supportive and lift the team up. Whether good or bad, you need to be able to openly discuss reality, especially when it comes to how your team supports each other. Looking out for each other is a foundation of working together and keeps team problems from arising.

FIVE MISTAKES OF FUZZY THINKING

> *Feelings are facts to the people feeling them.*
> –Henry J. Evans

I recently asked my team, "If I am silent about something you are doing, what does that mean to you?" To some, it means approval. Everything is OK. There's nothing to discuss. To others, it means disapproval. How can the silence of the leader, most often due to no opinion at all, have two such different meanings?

"Fuzzy thinking" is often self-imposed. It is created by some internal fear. Fear can be broken down into the acronym **FEAR: False Expectations Appearing Real.** These false expectations diminish self-esteem and can be classified as negative self-talk.

Negative self-talk could be, "I think she is going to fire me," when nothing could be further from the truth. It could be "I feel this small," which is an inaccurate self-evaluation. Such internal dialogs have nothing to do most often with the thoughts of the leader. These types of negative thought processes are best avoided, and should be replaced with positive self-talk. Such negative tendencies can affect the mind of a team member or even the leader. *Always remember that beliefs become fact only by evidence.*

In his book, *Leadership in 100 Days: Your Systematic Self-Coaching Roadmap to Power and Impact,* strategy and performance coach Dr. Thomas D. Zweifel discusses the pitfall of thinking that, "We know already." This attitude may preempt us from getting to the actual truth of a situation in an objective fashion. He calls this tendency "fuzzy thinking." See if any of these clouded thought processes ring true to you or remind you of someone on your team.

1. "IT'S TRUE BECAUSE WE BELIEVE IT."

Political groups and media have taken this mistake to new heights. The dominant beliefs of the group, even though they have never been questioned, studied, or verified, and are not supported by evidence or data, are the basis of beliefs, which are false. We call this "propaganda." Such beliefs can also be considered sociocentrism.

2. "IT'S TRUE BECAUSE I BELIEVE IT."

Do you have proof that what you think is true? The ego takes over. Innate egocentrism, or what you tell yourself, may not be true.

3. "IT'S TRUE BECAUSE I WANT TO BELIEVE IT."

This may be true of some individual or teams who think they are "the best" or otherwise "morally justified" in taking a certain action. Prove it! Humans tend to believe accounts that put them in a positive light, even though they have not considered the evidence. What "feels good" and does not change thinking, or make one have to admit that they have been wrong, becomes the belief. Therefore, the belief becomes an innate wish fulfilled.

4. "IT'S TRUE BECAUSE I HAVE ALWAYS BELIEVED IT."

Long-held beliefs are maintained until changed. This is also true for scientific "facts." The world is flat until proven round. Science is to be questioned.

5. "IT'S TRUE BECAUSE IT IS IN MY SELFISH SELF-INTEREST TO BELIEVE IT."

Some may hold to beliefs that help them gain power, money, or personal advantage. When the opportunity arises, they believe what benefits them, even when the belief is not based on sound reasoning or evidence.

QUESTION ALL SITUATIONS

Trust but verify.
–Ronald Reagan

As leaders, we must fight fuzzy thinking to counteract beliefs that are not founded on truth, evidence, and facts. This could be with your office, your team, your dental society, or even your government. When finding solutions to the issues being faced, *question incessantly.* This requires a high level of self-confidence to admit that although you don't have all the answers, you know that the team can solve any problem.

In dental practice management, it's essential to consider all frames of reference and all perspectives. Ask, "What could go wrong? What could go right? What are my assumptions? Am I basing my judgement on information that I have verified? Might I be biased or have blind spots to beliefs that I have never questioned before?"

Unquestioned assumptions or complacency can be perilous. **Verify that performance action items have actually been accomplished.** Verification is the job of a leader.

LOOK AT THE BIG PICTURE

If you think you are the entire picture,
you will never see the big picture.
–John C. Maxwell

There is a problem with the phrase, "Seeing is believing." Have you heard the story of the blind men who encountered an elephant? You can only draw a conclusion based upon what you can ascertain. Everyone's understanding is necessarily limited by their perspective. The leader's role is to **get all the information** so that you sense the big picture. Only then you will truly have a chance of knowing the elephant.

It's the same in your dental organization. At your team meeting, get all the information from everyone to assess what is going on and the direction in which you are heading. Then put all the pieces of the puzzle together. Only when you have all the data, can you start to draw a sound conclusion.

CASE STUDY 8: THE CONNOISSEUR

Franny was planning a social outing for her society. She did not know many of the older members who would attend. The dinner had a set fee, including wine. One older member had insisted that he not pay the wine fee.

Franny worried that perhaps the wine fee had offended the member. Perhaps drinking was against his religion. She hoped that he was not upset or uncomfortable at the dinner.

Fifteen years later, Franny finally learned by hearing the deceased member's homily that this member was, in fact, a wine connoisseur. He was known to bring his own wines to dinner from Napa, California.

Solution:

We all have biases which direct our thoughts in directions which may not be accurate. Don't assume. Ask. Verify.

SEVEN SIGNS THAT YOU NEED A LEADERSHIP ENERGY TUNE-UP

> *If you don't have it, you can't share it.*
> –Jon Gordon

Exceptional leaders are energetic. As leader, you will need to exercise, eat right, and get plenty of sleep. Find an activity that clears your mind and helps you relax so that you can be at peace at the end of a long day. My favorite out-of-the-office activities are gardening, making puzzles, and writing. Take time to rejuvenate yourself as a leader.

It is your responsibility as a leader to project "positive vibes." We can't do this if we are not energized, inspired, and positive. A leader cannot risk burnout. Just like a car, as a leader, you will need regular tune-ups in the form of coaching. Take this diagnostic test to see if you need to recharge your leadership batteries.

1. *You have difficulty getting started in the morning.*
2. *You feel that the pace of your life is too hectic.*
3. *You don't stop thinking about work, even when you go to bed.*
4. *You can't concentrate at work.*
5. *You don't spend enough time with your family.*
6. *You feel drained.*
7. *You dread going to work.*

If you said *yes* to any of these questions, it's time for a vacation and/ or a leadership tune-up. Take a break, get some mentoring, and gain some perspective.

Take control of the pace of your life. Make the important things in your life important. These usually include health, family, and friends. Slow down. Simplify your life.

Remember to put closure on each work day. Create time for daily rest. Watch a movie. Spend time with your family. Relax. Take a morning, afternoon, and evening break. Take a nap. Take time for rejuvenation of your mind, body, and soul.

TURN NEGATIVITY INTO GOLD

*There is little difference in people, but that little difference makes a
big difference.
The little difference is attitude. The big difference is
whether it is positive or negative.*
–W. Clement Stone

It is during the most difficult times that great things happen. Struggle inspires change and creativity. Like a diamond which becomes valuable through pressure, turn negativity into an opportunity for positive change. Whatever the situation, ask, **"What could be great about this?"**

If you look through history at the lives of great leaders, artists, and innovators, most had difficult life experiences. Nothing was handed to them. They worked for everything they earned. It can be the same for you.

Hardship can open many doors. Since the pandemic, I am now involved in a new study club which has been a positive influence on my life and career. Many such opportunities presented themselves during the pandemic. Many possibilities arose that led to fresh experiences and relationships that were enabled by the decision to "avoid Covid negativity."

Expressions of pessimism can also provide great opportunities to be of service to others. If someone speaks negatively, especially about a teammate, flip the conversation to ask how this venting can be turned into a positive action for themselves and change for the team.

Whining is OK, occasionally, as long as you offer a solution. Do not complain about a situation or teammate without simultaneously trying to remedy the situation. Help the teammate elevate their performance and attitude. Pick each other up. Have each other's backs. Help each other solve problems. This is the positive process of co-elevation.

Increase your own happiness and spread your own positive energy to those around you. In the end, if transforming the negativity doesn't work, you need to avoid or remove it.

Michelle Gielan speaks about the power of positive communication on YouTube and in her book, *Broadcasting Happiness*. As leader, you need to continuously share your optimism and belief in success. Look in the mirror each morning and ask yourself: "Are you ready to lead a successful team to achieve your goals? Are you grateful for the opportunity?" Feed yourself a positivity vitamin by thinking positive thoughts. Energize yourself so that you can inspire others.

Invest your energy in fulfilling activities which feed your soul and lead to enriching outcomes. What you choose to do needs to add meaning, enthusiasm, and joy to your life.

At no time was negativity more pronounced than during the pandemic. Some dental leaders looked at the lockdown and said, "I'm a health care provider, I'm essential. I'm still here for my patients, and I'll deal with it." Others self-destructed. Some gave up dental practice completely, sold out to corporate dentistry, or closed shop and retired.

During this challenging time, I asked my team, "Are we warriors, or are we victims?" We chose to be warriors. Everyone stayed active on the team and we cheered each other on. I gave two lockdown loyalty bonuses.

At the end of the pandemic, no team members were lost and our positive energy continued to fuel our success.

As a speaker, I usually get lots of feedback after a talk. My last American Association of Orthodontists (AAO) Annual Session's speaker score was 98.7 and I'm happy to be speaking again in 2023. But there is always that one bitterly negative comment. It's usually something like, "You're fat," or "This isn't marketing," or "You dodged a bullet!"

Don't take such negative comments personally. If you are a leader or a speaker, the target is you! Be happy that you can create something positive of your own and contribute to the world.

Chapter 6

ALIGNMENT

If everyone is moving forward together,
then success takes care of itself.

–Henry Ford

When words do not need to be spoken, when you and your staff work with one heart, and one mind, you know that you've achieved the biggest competitive advantage—an aligned team.

Some assistants can almost read my mind. We've worked together for so long, and done so many procedures together, that we know what to expect and what will happen next. This is the hallmark of an experienced assistant and great teamwork. Knowing what to expect and having total trust that we are here to work together while having each other's back, is the pinnacle of working together well.

Leading Dentists

The exceptional leader is like organized lightning,
with both a calming presence and an intensity
that raises the whole energy of the situations they engage.
–Allen Willet

You may have the opportunity to lead dentists. Take it. The dental profession needs great leaders. This is not an easy task, and at times it may feel like herding cats, but it can also be the honor of your lifetime. Take on this challenge to make your organization the best it can be by giving, serving, and leading.

A very talented orthodontist once asked me about membership in an orthodontic society. She asked, "Are the people nice?" This society had some members who were less than cheerful. It was not exactly known for friendliness, but it was a meritocracy and an honorary society worth joining. My answer to her was, "Someday, when you are on the board, then later president, you can work to make it the nicest it can be." She is now on the board and hospitality chair.

I am proud of how this group has been able to progress over the past twenty-five years. We have gone from a womanless organization to one reflecting the diversity of our profession and our country. By the introduction of new initiatives, we have accomplished innovative programs. Neglected details have been organized and systems improved. Social events and away meetings have been planned. Parliamentary procedures have been introduced and we have become more democratic. With rules of order come fairness and equal access. These were no small feats. For me personally, as a woman leader, it has been the most fulfilling professional journey of my lifetime.

Leadership Heart and Backbone Balance

A leader's ultimate test is how he or she copes in a crisis.
                                              –Thomas D. Zweifel

Leadership is not for the faint of heart. There will be tough times in which you will not only need a heart of gold but also a backbone of steel. **The most important thing that a leader can do is to never give up.** I hope that you will dive in and take the leadership challenge.

To be an effective leader, you must learn leadership skills. These include being supportive, encouraging, and nurturing. which requires heart. Demanding achievement requires backbone. You will be perfecting this balancing act your entire career. If you are only supportive and nurturing, you are a wimp; nothing will get done, and others will take advantage of you and your business. If you are bossy to the point of being a nag, your team will not follow you. If you force compliance, you will not be able to channel positive energy.

What you need as leader is the capability of being nurturing and demanding, sometimes simultaneously. You need to be a challenging supporter, someone not afraid to give both positive and critical feedback, and involved enough to know when either is required. Achieving this equilibrium is a leadership prerequisite.

How can you lead when you are having a difficult day yourself? Take full ownership of yourself and your role. Embrace the pain and work your way through it. To lead a team of leaders, it is necessary first to lead yourself.

Ask yourself, "Am I going to be an effective leader?" "Am I going to be an outstanding team member?" Start with yourself. Own it. The path to success is not straight. Don't choose to be mediocre. Don't be paralyzed by the pressures and pitfalls of leadership.

Three Team-Building Mistakes

In his book *Leading Teams,* Harvard Business School Professor J. Richard Hackman, one of the world's leading experts on organizational behavior, outlines the three biggest mistakes people make when they compose a team:

1.   *Assuming more is better.*
2.   *Composing a team which is too homogeneous.*
3.   *Paying too little attention to interpersonal skills.*

It is thought that the most ideal number of members for the highest performing team is four to five. High efficiency and teamwork drop off beyond five and most steeply when there are nine or more members.

You have been taught many things about leading a dental team by all the books you have read, all of the conversations that you have had with colleagues, and all the talks and podcasts to which you have listened. Stop waiting to be taught something that you already know. Can you be the best at what you do? Of course, you can.

Don't be overwhelmed by all the "experts." Next time you attend a dental CE meeting, ask yourself, "Has this person ever owned a dental office?" or "Has this person ever led a team?" You have instincts about what to do that are right for your situation. Use them. All the countless hours of work that you have done in your own dental office have created an internal resource that you can draw upon in any situation.

When Kobe Bryant was thirty-three years old, he was asked by a reporter at the 2012 Olympics in London if he could learn anything from the younger players. His response was, "No."

"You know everything?" the reporter asked.

"I don't know if I know it all," he responded, "but I know more than they do."

If you have studied your game your whole life, worked hard, and are a veteran, you know what maturity and experience have taught you. Instinct plus wisdom is priceless. If you are reading this book, it is my hope that it will help you further. Perhaps you already know what you need to do to improve your leadership or team. Just do it! You were just waiting for someone to boost your confidence. This is all you needed to move forward! **This is what a coach does: builds confidence.**

Now, I will tell you the two biggest mistakes that I ever made in my orthodontic practice over more than thirty years.

Mistake one: trying an office manager. It didn't work. The team got resentful as the manager was no longer part of the team. Now there was an extra level of inefficiency for you, the leader. Instead of just handling things yourself and getting things done, there's an unnecessary step. Unless you have over thirty people or are totally incapable of running your own dental practice or team meetings, you do not need an office manager.

Mistake two: not making patient-pending calls myself. This might be called relinquishing responsibility to a treatment coordinator or delegation. This small task, which takes less than two hours per week, has doubled my practice. Just last week, I scheduled seven new orthodontic starts. My return-on-investment for this activity was over $10,000 per hour (pretax). Why on earth would a dentist not spend time doing this themselves? I regret that I spent my early years and thousands of dollars on treatment coordinator training. After years of trial and error, I am happier, more fulfilled, and successful calling pending patients myself. Try it. You won't believe the results!

Yet I, like you, did not trust my own instincts. I listened to "experts." I lacked confidence. I tested different management methods. I experienced the results. Now there is no fear, no limitation. Just action and performance. Owning your personal leadership power is the most important tool that you will ever have in transforming the troublesome into the tremendous.

So, take control. Be organized. Own your leadership. As managers and leaders, we must never waiver in our obligation to the mission in which we are engaged. We must never give up on the group that we are leading. Sometimes this brings difficult decisions and tough love for the good of the group. This guidance always comes from compassion supported by the actions of a servant leader. Every time there is a troublesome situation, it is an opportunity to help someone or something grow—the organization, the team, and perhaps even ourselves—while gaining wisdom about dental practice management and leadership in the process.

Your Leadership Philosophy

> *Philosophy drives attitude. Attitude drives actions.*
> *Actions drive results. Results drive lifestyles.*
> —Jim Rohn

Your "why" is your philosophy. Why do you do what you do? As a leader, you will have a philosophy which will drive your attitude and your actions. You may not know what your philosophy is yet. Take a few minutes to write down what is most compelling and important to you in your life.

My personal philosophy would read:

To be the best mom and wife that I can be. To be the best orthodontist that I can be. To contribute in a positive way to others in my family, in my profession, in my office, in my communities, and in the world. To have work-life balance.

Women in Leadership

> *There is a special place in hell*
> *for women who don't help other women.*
> —Madeleine Albright

I was fortunate to have attended all-women's Wellesley College, the alma mater of Madeleine Albright, Hillary Clinton, Cokie Roberts, and many other famously strong women. Our school motto is, *"Non Ministrari sed Ministrare"*—not ministered but to minister. Here we learned to be independent, ambitious, assertive, and to support other women. This experience has served me well in my lifetime.

I was also fortunate to have attended Harvard School of Dental Medicine, being graduated in 1988. At that time, the orthodontic department had some outstanding women orthodontists. Dr. Carla Evans was my instructor. A leader in the orthodontic field, she served as acting chairman of the orthodontic department. She later moved to the University of Illinois, where she served as chairman of orthodontics for nearly twenty years. I had the pleasure of personally speaking with her again at the Angle Society Biennial Meeting in 2021. She is now semiretired but still teaching at Boston University. Carla Evans is a true woman leader in orthodontics, a trailblazer, and an inspiration to me and to all women orthodontists. Seeing her again at this meeting was one of the highlights of my professional life.

During my orthodontic residency program at Northwestern University, there were no women instructors. I remember the feeling that first day in 1988 when I arrived and realized that the six orthodontic residents a year ahead of me were all men, and that all of my classmates were also men. My heart sank. These guys ended up being like brothers to me. Nonetheless, it created a feeling of being an outsider in my own profession.

When I began teaching at the University of California San Francisco in 1991, there was one other female orthodontic department member, Dr. Karin Vargervik. She served as acting chairman for a few years during transition to a new department chairman. This was the orthodontic world that I experienced early on.

Years later, I was determined to join an orthodontic society, which was a difficult journey, as I became the first woman admitted to this group. But I am happy to say that, more than twenty-five years later, after many trials and tribulations, I am now the first woman president. I am determined to be supportive and an encourager of all other women dentists working toward leadership positions.

For the first ten years in the organization, I experienced limited collegiality. One day a very nice member, Dr. Ken Kai, a past president of the Pacific Coast of Orthodontists, asked me, "How have things been for you here?"

I told him, "This has not been as rewarding as I might have expected." That day, he invited me to attend the next board of directors meeting. It was in that moment, having been given a chance to be of service to the organization, that everything changed.

Shortly thereafter, I presented a list of thirty-five names of potential new candidates for membership. Many of these talented orthodontists have now joined the society. When I look out at the present board, I see people, almost all of whom were on my list, and I am filled with gratitude and satisfaction that I have contributed to diversity and have made a difference.

I urge other ascent women to support women in their struggle toward equality, inclusion, and ascent to leadership positions. Don't be an "Auntie Tom," trying to please when inappropriate, or a "Door Mat," doing all the work that others do not want to do while not assuming leadership. Speak up in order to build a most just and inclusive society.

Speak Up

> We stand in a circle whose circumference is bounded by
> the circle of our own fears.
> –Mahatma Gandhi

For a woman leader, opportunities don't come easily. Deep down, you know that staying the course and keeping quiet may not lead you to a desired goal, yet doing so may avoid the uncomfortable situation of fighting for what you feel is best. Ask yourself: "Will I regret what I didn't do or what I didn't say? Will I regret not speaking up?"

In her book *How Remarkable Women Lead: The Breakthrough Model for Work and Life,* author Joanna Barsh MBA, New York City Commissioner of Women's Issues and a former Baker Scholar at Harvard Business School, states that *for women leaders, forestalling risk is not an option.*

Women are more reluctant to take risks than men. The reason for this is unclear. Perhaps women like keeping the peace and bearing the pain. I recently had a female colleague tell me she thought being a woman was an asset in orthodontic leadership because not speaking up has kept her out of trouble. But, incessantly, doing the work of others while not having a leadership position is not heroic. Ships in the harbor are safe. But that is not what ships are for.

It is true, women are less likely to have powerful sponsors in an organization. They also have less support from other women. Whether you're a woman or a man, nothing ventured, nothing gained. Resist the desire to head back to your comfort zone, and head forward into expanded leadership capacity for the betterment of your organization, yourself, and the world.

Women often think, "They will make fun of me." Yes, men (and other women) will. But, by doing so, others make fools of themselves. Look right in the eye of this worst-case scenario and take the risk. You can be a capable, strong leader.

You're ready to face risks and fears. Ask for what you want. I guess I was just born not being afraid to ask. I've always asked myself this question: "What's the worst that can happen?" When you're faced with a situation where, if you do nothing, then nothing will happen for you, you have nothing to lose by asking the next question to open the door of opportunity.

CASE STUDY 9: LITTLE MISS BOLD

Hannah's short, five-year-old legs hung down from the office chair. Her white knee socks emphasized her black patent leather shoes. She knew this was a very important interview for kindergarten admission. The nun in her habit looked at Hannah and her father sternly at the application interview.

The nun explained to Hannah's father that they were not church parishioners. The principal barely had enough space in the elementary school for the children of families in her own parish. This school did not have room for Hannah, and the nun's answer for admission was going to have to be, "No."

Hannah looked over at her father. She thought he was going to cry. Hannah knew that her mother, an elementary school principal, wanted her to go to this fine school. Hannah's local public school had no kindergarten. Hannah's father gestured to Hannah, "Let's go."

Hannah quickly spoke. "Sister, are you aware that I am the Massachusetts state piano playing champion in my age group?"

The sister replied, "Is that so? Would you like to play something for me right now?"

Hannah replied, "Yes, I would!"

They proceeded to the school auditorium. Determined, Hannah walked up the steps to the piano on the stage. She sat down and confidently played, "Dance of the Trolls."

Arriving back home, the phone rang. Hannah's dad answered. Hannah was accepted! After the school year started, Hannah played a recital on the stage for the entire student body.

Solution:

A single moment of speaking up can change your entire life. There is no downside to speaking up. Seek, and you shall find. Knock, and the door will be opened for you. Ask, and you shall receive.

THE ACHILLES' HEEL OF WOMEN LEADERS

> *The challenge we all face as leaders is*
> *to let the feelings churn inside you*
> *but then to present a calm exterior,*
> *and I learned to do that.*
>
> –Indra Nooyi

In moments of intense emotion, a man will get angry. He may yell, swear, even pound his fists on the table. He will demand control and attention. He will fight to get what he wants.

A woman will experience the need to cry. An upset woman will need to fight to hold back her tears. This is true of every woman leader. When this happens to you as a woman leader, it is perhaps best to excuse yourself and leave the room.

I was comforted to read that as CEO of PepsiCo, Indra Nooyi would have times when she would go into her office bathroom and just cry. I found it consoling to know that no matter how successful you are as a woman leader, no matter how big your company or how many people you lead, you still retain the sensitive, female qualities of expression.

There will be times in your dental practice when you will feel the physiological need to cry. At these times, collect yourself. Stop the meeting for the day. Walk out, if necessary. Take a break. Take a deep breath and calm down. Then start over.

Reappear stronger than before and exclaim, "Let's get cracking!" You may not be able to win every battle, but you can give it another try. My dad would always tell me, "A winner never quits, and a quitter never wins." I still have that sign from my dad hanging in my office.

THE FUTURE

> *True leaders must keep their feet firmly rooted to the ground*
> *and focus on the responsibilities of their jobs.*
> –Indra Nooyi

I have always tried to focus on where I might be able to make a contribution. Whatever task I take on, I would like to make things better for my organization, profession, office, or family. I have the attitude, "Let's roll up our sleeves and get to work."

Where there is meritocracy and ethics, women have an equal opportunity. Although slow in many areas, progress is palpable. Minorities and newer Americans are also moving forward and upward. America still is the land of opportunity.

Women dentists are fortunate to run their own offices, choose their own hours, and work for pay equal to any male colleague. We are able to bring our whole selves to work, feel comfortable, and steer our business in the way we deem best. In this regard, dentistry is perhaps one of the best professions for women. We have the leadership opportunity to be CEOs of our own destiny.

Presently, 7.5 percent of Fortune 500 companies are led by women CEOs, referred to as "breaking the glass ceiling." There are, however, plenty of chances for women to take over in times of crisis, or to do work that others do not want to do. This is called the "glass cliff." Many women leaders have engineered tremendous turnarounds through this opportunity.

Many women need to take the ultimate step of assuming actual leadership. There is no need to settle to be the secretary-for-life. Do not acquiesce to whomever is the loudest politician. Don't just do what you're told. Take center stage. Yes, you will have challenges. People may trip you up, talk over you, or even take control of your Zoom screen during meetings! There will never be a good time to be a leader. You will always have a family and extra responsibilities. The world needs women leaders now. Don't let yourself be passed over for a leadership opportunity by taking yourself out of contention. Remember, you *are* a leader and you can continue to be a leader no matter how loud the noise around you gets.

Succession Planning

> *More female leaders will mean a*
> *healthier, wealthier, more egalitarian society.*
> –Indra Nooyi

When I joined the Northern California Angle Society as the first woman member more than twenty-five years ago, I figured that it would probably take an equal amount of time for this group to become balanced with equal numbers of men and women orthodontists. I am happy to state that today, we have equal numbers of males and females on the board, and our membership appears to be growing with equal gender representation. I am confident that leadership opportunities will improve as women continue to lean in and speak up in the coming years.

In her book *My Life in Full*, Indra Nooyi relates that, in her lifetime, corporate America has gone from two percent women CEOs to 7.5 percent. At this rate, it will take 130 years to reach gender equality. She states that the CEO pipeline is leaky for women. Due to additional commitments such as child and elder care, women often fall out of the line of succession. Once you fall off the conveyor belt, it's hard to get back on.

For women to continue to rise in leadership, they will need the courage to speak up and be direct in their firm desire to assume the mantle of leadership. Women will need to demand ethical and professional behavior in the organizations for which they serve. They will need to continue to work for diversity, equity, inclusion, and belonging. Women also need support from other women.

Whether as leader of your orthodontic office or president of your society, one of your key jobs as a leader will be succession planning. Have a plan and begin training your replacement. As leader, you will always be dealing with the people puzzle. As leader, you can also prepare for your future replacement.

Indra Nooyi stated that the best advice she ever received was this: "The distance between number one and number two is a constant." When a leader overperforms, the team comes along with him or her; when the leader underperforms, the same thing happens. So, stay on top of your game, serve, and run for a leadership position. Leadership is service. Those serving are already leaders. They might as well get the official office.

There is no letting up on leadership until the last hour of the last day of your term. Similarly, in your dental practice, there is no letting up until the day that you retire.

EXPERIENCE

In 1896, Henry Ford was a thirty-three-year-old engineer at Detroit Edison. At the annual meeting, the conversation turned to electric-powered vehicles. Ford had just completed his "Quadricycle." With great fervor, the world-famous inventor Thomas A. Edison brought his fists to the table and declared, "Young man, you have it. Keep at it." Three years later Ford struck out on his own, making gasoline-powered carriages. Ford later explained that "his bang on the table was worth worlds to me. No man up until then had given me any encouragement." The two builders became lifelong friends.

As you step up into your leadership position, you will find supporters as well as detractors. Embrace your supporters. Ignore your non-supporters. Try to enlist those who are neutral. Ignore those who remain negative. In the words of Bernie Stoltz, CEO of Fortune Management, it's "Win/Win or Bye/Bye." Make sure you are involved in co-elevating relationships.

The only way for any person to learn leadership is simply to lead. You will learn by experience. You will learn from your mistakes. I find inspiration in leadership from listening to the wise words of great leaders on

YouTube and reading their biographies. Their optimistic outlook is invigorating. What you will face is common and has been experienced by all leaders.

Stay in your leadership zone and stay persistently positive. Have a heart of gold but a backbone of steel. We must all learn to work together to create the successful future that we seek.

You cannot control the actions of other people but you can work every day to set a good example so as to influence others. You can only control yourself. Don't take other people's actions personally. Work to understand the psychology space that surrounds you. If you are the leader, you might be blamed for the actions of others in your group. So be it. Your job as leader is to sustain the good of your organization and keep it viable. No matter how difficult it may seem, keep asking, "How could we work together?"

Chapter 7

ACTION

The older I get the less I listen to what people say
and the more I look at what they do.
–Andrew Carnegie

A s a leader, your responsiveness to making decisions, assigning tasks, and working out details determines your success. A tone of urgency is needed in order to take action. As leader, hold people accountable for what they are assigned to do. Let everyone know that there is no time to waste.

PLAN YOUR YEAR

We may be very busy, we may be very efficient,
but we will also be truly effective only when
we begin with the end in mind.
–Stephen R. Covey

As leader, you may be asking yourself, "Where do I start?" Begin with an annual advance planning meeting for your team. The yearly advance (not retreat!) puts your big picture business plan front and center for everyone to see. In this way, you are creating the game plan first, prior to implementation.

Define what you are trying to accomplish. Get organized, bringing everyone on board. Plan your year. You can modify your plans as you go, but the general outline, built during your advance, guides you in the desired direction.

To aid in each team member's engagement for the annual advance, distribute a questionnaire ahead of time. Here is a sample of what you could include:

Four Annual Advance Questions

1. *What do you think were our team's greatest accomplishments of the past year?*
2. *What was your finest personal achievement during the past year?*
3. *What will you do differently in the coming year to make the practice more successful?*
4. *What are your expectations for our annual advance and the coming year?*

The annual advance prepares a big-picture view of the office business plan. Here is a sample outline of an annual advance agenda.

Annual Advance Agenda
Continental Breakfast   9:00 a.m.
Doctor   9:30 a.m.
    Introduction
    Vision, Mission, Core Values, Tagline
    Questionnaire results   10:00 a.m.
    SWOT analysis
        (Strengths, Weaknesses, Opportunities, Threats)
Treatment Coordinator   10:30 a.m.
    Year-End Report
    Average exams/month
    Average starts/month
    Same-day starts/month
    Goals for the coming year

Public Relations Coordinator	11:00 a.m.
Year-End Report	
Total number of referrals	
Number of referrals from doctors, breakdown	
External marketing referrals and analysis	
Internal marketing referrals	
Marketing calendar for the coming year	
Team	11:30 a.m.
Brainstorming	
Lunch	12:00 p.m.
Financial Coordinator	1:00 p.m.
Year-End Report	
Accounts receivable: responsible parties	
Accounts receivable: insurance	
Accounts payable	
Records Coordinator	1:30 p.m.
Customer service update, reviews	
Schedule update for the next week, month, 90 days, year	
Doctor	2:00 p.m.
HR and Handbook updates	
Courses and special events for the coming year	
Goals for the coming year	
Team	3:00 p.m.
Brainstorming	
Doctor	
Achievement awards	3:30 p.m.
Meeting adjourned	4:00 p.m.

SWOT ANALYSIS

The SWOT analysis—Strengths, Weaknesses, Opportunities, and Threats—serves as a chance to gain necessary perspectives about the office, your success, plans, and what to work on together. The SWOT analysis lays groundwork for brainstorming and action plans for the coming year.

Plan Your Day

> *Either you run the day or the day runs you.*
> –Jim Rohn

Ask yourself, "What is the most important thing that I need to accomplish today?" Write it down. Then make sure to accomplish that *one* thing.

Watch your minutes and day, and the week will take care of itself. The month will flow. The year will follow. Focus on the now, and what you can achieve today, and you will always be rewarded.

Daily accountability is reflected on the end-of-day sheet. What was today's production? What were today's collections? Did we have new-patient exams? Is there cash to be delivered to the bank? Did the end-of-day sheet deposit match the bank deposit the next morning?

Verification of the end-of-day sheet is a vital responsibility of the business owner. This is not micromanagement. It is attention to details and systems which will make your office successful.

Plan Your Week

> *Nothing, and no one, can disrupt your intention.*
> –Thomas D. Zweifel

It is at the weekly team meeting that you clarify what is the most important focus of the coming week. In our office, everyone speaks and remains engaged. One team member reports the appointment openings remaining for the next week. This gives you a chance to fill these slots. Review lead measures of what can still be done, not lag measures of past reports of previous weeks about which you can do nothing.

If extra space is needed for new-patient starts, you can add doctor time to the weekly schedule. I often remind my team, "You are in total control. There is no need to be stressed. You are in charge of our schedule. If something needs to be altered, we will change it." The key is to know, and be clear about your own office priorities.

Maintaining laser focus means discarding "junk experiences." Time wasters may include an unwanted company lunch. Cancel it. That time could be better used, even if to relax or make patient or referring doctor calls. Always emphasize practice building activities.

I like to wrap up my week with the team meeting on the last day. We hold our team meetings from 12:00 p.m. to 1:00 p.m. on Thursdays. No food, just focus, discussion, and engagement. Once the meeting is over, we break for lunch until 2:30 p.m. We finish our day at 6:00 p.m., ready for the week ahead, fresh and prepared.

Start your week with momentum and ten phone calls: ten new patients that you want to start, or ten new dentists with whom you want to work, or ten businesses with whom you would like to partner. Make important payments on Mondays. If you have a loan, keep a goal of making a payment every Monday until the loan is paid off. It's only the first hour of your week, and look how much you have already accomplished!

Train everyone to "own" their schedule, "own" their column of patients, "own" their week, "own" their team wins, and "own" their future. Start your week having something special to anticipate. Make it a great week! You've got this!

I keep my monthly year calendar on my desk. I also keep the calendar from the past year to remind myself what really worked well in the past. Look at the months and year ahead. Does your office have any special events planned? Are there any days off or meetings to be attended? Will your PR director be making deliveries? Does the doctor have lunches with colleagues or CE events? Whatever you do as a team, even if it is as simple as sending Christmas cards, can and should be programmed at the weekly team meeting.

Cash Flow

> *He who does not honor the cent is not worth the dollar.*
> —Swiss Proverb

It's the last day of the month. Your last patient has left. You are prepared to start the new month. You may have a target balance, which you would like to maintain to cover your next rent or mortgage payment and payroll, including the doctor's salary. Do you have a surplus or do you have a few bills left to pay? If you have a few bills, assuming that you worked as well as you could, you need to reduce costs.

Share the end-of-the-month situation with the team. I assume that all workers want raises. To have sufficient funds, increase collections and reduce expenses. Cash flow is not production. *A dentist can work themselves to death with production and still have poor cash flow if collections and expenses are not under control.* Collections need to be maximized. Expenses need to be as low as possible.

When leaders feel that "menial details" like cash flow are beneath them, that is when systems start to break down. Every metric reflects strategic intent. All numbers are relevant to the business owner. At the heart of profitability are the details.

Attention to cash flow is essential for proper functioning of dental societies. Not reading contracts carefully, ignoring costs, or overspending the budget are examples of irresponsible actions that reflect poorly on all board members. Remember that the main responsibility of the board beyond running the organization is financial oversight.

MAKE MONEY MATTERS CLEAR

> *There's no such thing as a free lunch.*
> –Milton Friedman

With open-book management, all money matters are shared with the entire office. Whether collections are up or down, the number is the result of the team effort. Whether it's a raise year or not is reflected by collections and should be no surprise to anyone. Open-book management takes financial pressure off the owner/leader while building the trust and engagement of the staff. The team's success is in their own hands. They've earned it themselves. They know that the pay, bonuses, and raises are fair.

Take time to talk about money with your team. This may not be easy for the younger dentists, but it is a necessary skill that will come more naturally with practice and maturity. Explain the 401(k) retirement plan.

Explain paid vacations and holidays. Order a new team uniform. These are the benefits not every job offers. Let the interviewee and team members know that, $17.25 at Amazon or $22 at McDonald's does not equal $17.25 working full time in a dental office with benefits.

By understanding and appreciating money matters, employees become more secure in their jobs. Let the team know that you don't reduce pay or hours to cut costs. The corresponding responsibility is that, *as a team, together, you watch expenditures and price check to keep the office profitable.*

Before you call in your payroll hours, have each team member review their hours for accuracy, and initial that their time sheet is correct. This could save you time and money in the future by avoiding a payroll audit. Overtime is always paid when due and payroll is always accurate. Go over payroll dates with your team as explained in the Team Handbook. Define how weekend and holiday pay dates will be handled.

Our Team Handbook lists pay dates of the 5th and the 20th. These dates apply to pay time periods 1–15th, and 15th–31st. Payroll may come before the 5th and the 20th of each month, but it will never come after that date.

Winning for the team is often equated with financial rewards. There are two ways to grow the surplus: increase production/collections, or reduce expenses. Remember:

PROFIT = COLLECTIONS - EXPENSES

Profit is your team's salary and the doctor's salary. Profit is the reward for hard work and careful cash management. Your profit is your reward for working well together. Paradoxically, "people-over-profits" workplace culture most often increases the bottom line. With the right people, and the right spirit, monies are not wasted and the profits follow.

Notice that I am not listing production here. Production numbers might give the practice owner and team an unrealistic picture of financial success. Although production numbers can be a harbinger of future revenues, **collections are what really matter.** Collections are cash flow, the fuel of your practice engine. Stated another way, production without collection is charity work.

Therefore, one ratio to concentrate on is the collections to production ratio. You want this as close to 100 percent as possible, at least in the high nineties. Watch this number as an indicator of control of discounting and attention to accounts receivable from patients and insurance carriers.

No office can afford to be doing dental treatment for free. You pay for the supplies, labor, and overhead costs. Take care to get a substantial down payment before starting treatment. Always have a signed financial contract and an accepted treatment plan.

Payment contracts augment informed consent for the patient as well. No dentist wants to be perceived as providing care that the patient did not want. Take time to explain the treatment plan and the financial arrangements. Always start treatment after having medical clearance, treatment consent, and patient financial contracts signed by both the patient and the doctor.

CONTROLLED SPENDING

> *A penny saved is a penny earned.*
> –Benjamin Franklin

Push back against quick decisions or consensus on a bad idea. This is especially true with overspending and not reading contracts. If you are leading a nonprofit dental board, make sure everyone on the board has a copy of the contract under consideration and for full review and discussion before anyone makes the decision to sign. **Always make sure that your contract is not open-ended.** A closed contract gives the final total cost and does not continue charging by the hour *ad infinitum.* Once you sign a contract, it will be difficult to reverse it, if not impossible to reverse it. If you have questions about a contract, have your attorney review it before signing.

Financial push back in a group setting requires a careful balance of using political influence as well as depending on self-reliance. Don't avoid discussion and just hope for the best. Wishful thinking can only lead to disaster. I remember once our building tenant's association wanted to sue our landlord. Emotions got the best of the group. I had to walk away from what appeared to be a dangerous open-ended financial precipice. I hired my own attorney and renegotiated my lease in what turned out to be an excellent money-saving decision. If you need help with lease renegotiation, contact George Vaill at www.dentalleasenegotiations.com. Initiate talks two years ahead of the lease renewal due date.

The best thing that I ever did to control spending in my office was get my own mail and review my own invoices, which can be organized by due date. This will give you a clear understanding of cash flow on a daily basis. Bills come with plenty of mistakes. Just this week I received an invoice for toothbrushes costing $300 with a shipping charge of $203! I doubted that was correct. I called the company and the cost was reduced to $20.30! It will save you thousands of dollars to accounts payable for accuracy.

Share costs with your team. Let them know the cost of equipment, ADA dues, and Invisalign. ***Once your team understands your expenses, costs will be contained and there will be no urge for unnecessary spending.*** Once the inventory coordinator documents supply costs, she can start comparison shopping to find the best price possible. A suction tip is a suction tip! They all work. Cost is the overriding consideration.

The second-best thing I ever did in my office to control spending was to get my inventory coordinator her own credit card with a limit of $1,500. This facilitates acquisition of items bought locally, such as distilled water for the sterilizer, or similar inventory. It also provides an ongoing appreciation of how quickly costs add up. With this knowledge, the inventory coordinator can price check, just as she would with her own money.

A few of my colleagues expanded to a second location in the roaring 2000s. Just a few years later, during the recession of 2008, they ended up closing their second location after incurring financial losses. A second office can definitely be a huge and unnecessary expense.

Case Study 10: The Executive Director

The board was planning a national meeting. One board member had volunteered to run the meeting and chair the planning committee. Once appointed, he announced, "I need an executive director." I thought, "Shoot, if I had known that I could hire an executive director, I would have volunteered!"

The board voted that the executive director would be paid $10,000 to run the three-day meeting. This was a steep fee considering that hotels have event planners as part of the reservation package to help organize functions at a lower cost. Nonetheless, the $10,000 fee was voted on and passed by the board. A few months later, it was announced at a board meeting that the fee would now be $16,000. Board members squirmed. One asked, "Could I see the contract?"

It was an open-ended contract that charged by the hour with no limit. Now the executive director had hired his own assistant and was charging for her services as well!

When all was done, the group paid the executive director $30,000 for a three-day meeting! The final payment was three times the original estimate and there was nothing that could be done about it.

Solution:

Read contract proposals carefully. Never sign an open-ended contract. Don't rush into decisions that have not been thoroughly examined and discussed. Have a very low threshold for consulting your attorney on contracts.

TEN ACTS OF LEADERSHIP

Leaders don't run away from problems. Leaders run toward them. The sooner you solve problems, the faster you will achieve success.

Here are ten leadership actions to embrace.

1. *LEAN INTO DISCOMFORT*

> *You can choose courage or you can choose comfort,*
> *but you can't have both.*
>
> –Brené Brown

Most of us don't like to confront others, especially when they are making our lives difficult. As leader, it is your job to initiate corrective action. Sometimes dental leaders are just too darn nice. Sometimes we're afraid of an uncomfortable conversation to highlight an unwanted behavior.

Raise the standards for yourself, your team, and our profession by undertaking necessary discussions.

Do not fear rejection. No matter what you do, there will be someone to criticize and reject you. Swallow your fear and press for a solution. Sometimes it will work. Sometimes it will not. It is your job as leader to at least give it a try.

2. CARE THAT ALL IS DONE RIGHT

Your team might be waiting for you to dive in and get more involved before they put in the extra effort. "That's not my job" should never be stated by anyone on your team, least of all by the leader. Owners of dental practices are usually the last out the door at night and perhaps the first to arrive in the morning. Never demand anything of your team that you are not willing to do yourself. Lead by example.

Take responsibility for assigning the right person to the right job. Proper delegation is in the owner's wheelhouse. Assign important tasks to the best person for each and every task at hand.

3. MAKE CO-ELEVATION YOUR STANDARD

You will never know or be able to control what goes on in another person's mind. Perhaps they have been bullied or discriminated against. Once you become leader, work toward cooperation, unity, and a better future.

Some team members may quit under your leadership, blaming you or the office for their lack of commitment. Let them leave. That's their choice. Don't take it personally. They may not have the same standards or work ethic that you do. They did the group a favor by letting you know that they don't want to be on your team.

Don't get caught up in how things were or the anti-leadership statement, "We've always done it this way." You are the leader now. This is your time to lead. Don't let anything or anyone hold you back from being fantastic. Encouragement is the greatest motivator for both you and your team. Be a force for good. Begin a movement of co-elevation.

4. *Make Decisions Quickly*

> *Every leader has the courage to make decisions.*
> *No decision is usually the worst decision.*
> –Orrin Woodward

Time is money. Don't waste your time or your money. You don't want to discuss things twice. Discuss things once, make a decision, and get on with it.

5. *Be Informed*

Whatever is going on in your organization, you, as the leader, should know about it. Ignorance is not an excuse for a leader. If you don't know something, ask. Be vigilant. Take time to confirm. Do not assume anything. Start with an open-ended question, such as, "How is it going?" Then, listen. I have found that saying, "What can I do to help you?" is demeaning to some people. In their book *Work with Me,* authors Barbara Annis and John Gray state that unsolicited help indicates to a man that he is not trusted or capable of accomplishing the job on his own. It is better to say, "Let's work together to improve this situation."

It didn't take me long to realize that my staff is full of great ideas. Your own team could be the best consultant that you ever had. Get them talking. Your own office sees things that you don't see. They know things that you don't know. Patients open up to team members and give suggestions for improvements. Be each team member's biggest listener and cheerleader.

6. *Be Involved*

A leader needs to be accessible. This is why, when I designed my orthodontic office, I placed my personal office right in the center. My door is always open and I can see everything going on in the practice, so that I can be as involved as possible.

A team will appreciate seeing the owner working hard. This will build confidence in leadership ability. The dentist should never be too busy to make sure that the most important jobs are done. If you feel that you are too busy for leadership, cut activities to save time. Whatever needs to be accomplished, you are there to lead it, implement it, organize it, or, when necessary, do it.

7. COMMUNICATE FREQUENTLY

> *Communication is the real work of leadership.*
> –Nitin Nohria

Silence isn't golden. It's deadly. Howard Farran, founder of Dentaltown and Orthotown, in his podcast "Dentistry Uncensored" often states that he can tell a successful dental office the moment he walks in because people are talking and laughing.

Humor + A Smile = Collaboration

Keep the lines of communication open: leader to team, team member to team member, team member to leader. Ease of communication is the hallmark of great collaboration, teamwork, and leadership.

Stay current with your team. As your team members communicate on each new situation, listen so that you are well-informed. You cannot afford to be out of the loop. Ask daily, "Is there anything new?"

The greatest strength of a leader is their ability to listen. Listen to suggestions at team meetings and let team members talk without cutting them off. Consider every proposal. Seek first to understand, then to be understood.

8. PRAISE PUBLICLY

> *Praise in public; criticize in private.*
> –Vince Lombardi

Never criticize a team member in public. This is perhaps the most important rule of leadership. People are extremely sensitive. When necessary, ask, "May I speak to you for a moment in my office?" Take a deep breath. Say, "Next time, would you be able to do it this way?"

Your team members have pride in themselves and their work. They try their best. It is your responsibility as a leader to coach them and make them successful. A display of public negativity may lead to loss of dignity for the individual and respect for the leader. It might even result in separation of a valued team member. Do the opposite. Praise publicly.

9. BE FAIR

> *People in your organization want to be*
> *treated fairly and with compassion.*
> *It's not a lot to ask.*
>
> –Joan Garry

Some people are higher performers than others. Some may be more likeable. But as leader, you must treat everyone on your team equally with the same respect. *Lack of fairness leads to resentment and loss of morale.* This is especially true on teams of volunteer dental organizations.

You want each person to feel welcomed and great about their service to the organization. This is another reason why the Policies and Procedures, Team Handbook, and Bylaws are so important. Rules of your organization need to be followed by everyone equally. Fairness sets the tone of your culture as one of inclusivity and belonging.

10. NEVER GIVE UP

> *I believe in running a company for the*
> *shareholders that are going to stay,*
> *rather than ones who are going to leave.*
>
> –Warren Buffet

It will be hard, if not impossible, to ever find anyone as dedicated to your dental practice as you, the owner. If you are president of your organization, others may quit, but you cannot. Accept this reality and you will never be disappointed. As the leader, you will be facing difficult challenges. Resolution of challenges is the job of a leader. That leader is you.

You have worked hard to buy, run, or start a dental practice. Be grateful to have your practice and enjoy its benefits. You strived and served your society to rise in the ranks. Whatever you are experiencing as leader, there is no time for "Why me?" thinking. You have total freedom and control over how you react to every situation. Choose to be brave, smart, strong, and effective.

THE EXCEPTIONAL LEADER

Whatever you can do or dream you can do... Begin it.
Boldness has genius, power, and magic in it. Begin it now.
–Johann Wolfgang von Goethe

Exceptional leaders look into the mirror knowing, "If it is to be, it's up to me." These leaders look at problems as opportunities. They are not discouraged by obstacles. They think that the leadership challenges are fun.

Every leader can get better. Choose the path of lifelong learning. Look for mentors, role models, and coaches. Read. Just by reading this book you have improved. Listen to leadership podcasts on YouTube. Never stop learning.

Take ownership of your leadership position. You've worked hard to get there. You're prepared. You're confident. You can handle any situation. Take pride in yourself and your accomplishments.

As leaders, we must never waiver from our obligation to the mission and to the group we lead. In the words of legendary leader Alan Mulally: "Love'm Up!" The exceptional leader looks at challenges, solves them, and continues to take the best actions to achieve success. She carries on with strategic intent, sticking with the core values of the organization. She never gives up.

The concept of Constant And Never-Ending Improvement (CANI) gets me out of bed in the morning, and has inspired me to write this book for you. It motivates me to work with exceptional coaches and follow exceptional leaders. I have probably made more leadership mistakes than most people, but I've learned from them. The basic task of leadership is to increase the quality of life for all stakeholders. Choose this path with joy and live in abundance.

Chapter 8

COURAGE

A great leader's courage to fulfill his vision
comes from passion, not position.

–John C. Maxwell

M aintaining courage during emotionally charged discussions is perhaps the most difficult part of running a dental practice. It's OK to be the boss. In fact, you need to step up and be the boss if you own your practice. You have taken financial risks and earned the right to be leader. As part of your role, you will face pushback on change, challenges on rule enforcement, and resistance to new initiatives. You may even hear the cop-out response, "Don't micromanage me." Expect it and deal with it effectively. This responsibility goes hand-in-hand with the privilege of business ownership.

It is rare in practice and in life that all will be perfect. CEO Jack Welch said it best: "Every day, there is a new challenge." There will be crisis and unexpected events. At these times, remember that you are the captain of the ship. You have a clear vision of where you are going. That is your destination. You are adaptable in how you get there. There will be winds altering your course. Summon the courage to lead your team through the storm.

Handle challenges head-on, with confidence. The sooner that you deal with your problems and come up with solutions, the sooner you will achieve success.

Leadership is marked by bold decisions. Whether as owner of a dental office, or officer of a dental society, the leader will need to work decisively to move the organization's trajectory in a positive direction.

The leader is at the edge of the group, out in front. *The leader is not in the pack. The leader will not initially have consensus.* **A leader will always be at the edge of consensus.** The leader works to build the consensus of the followers.

A Leader Stands Alone

Leaders should be able to
Stand Alone, Take the Heat, Bear the Pain, Tell the Truth,
and Do What's Right.
–Max DePree

Have no doubt about it, leaders personally suffer to make needed change. Just think of Gandhi, Lincoln, Kennedy, Reagan, Pope John Paul II, or Jesus. Three assassinations, two assassination attempts, and a crucifixion. It is not an easy path to be an outstanding leader.

Leaders put the issues out in the open in order to solve them. Solutions are found by honest, truthful, and transparent discussion, no matter how initially unpopular the subject. Resolution is achieved by candor, which means taking risks and taking action.

It's the leader's job in the dental practice or society to see that necessary changes get accomplished. These course corrections may not initially be deemed important by everyone. "That's how we've always done it around here" is a typical mantra used against a leader seeking a new direction.

Others have not had your experiences. They have not viewed human behavior through your set of eyes. All of your life experiences contribute to your leadership style. Don't expect that your ideas and initiatives will automatically be understood or appreciated by all. Others see the world through their own lenses. So, don't wait to be appreciated, appreciate. Don't let your difficulties define you, let them inspire you to reach out to others. This is the job of a leader. To give and to serve. ***There is no quitting for a leader.***

A Leader Accepts Reality

Tough leadership decisions may include initiating an ethics committee, creating a diversity, equity, and inclusion (DEI) taskforce, cutting costs, starting new projects, beginning or ending partnerships, building fiduciary oversight, establishing transparency and fairness, or eliminating a dysfunctional team member. All of these examples are difficult. But change is necessary to create organizational systems to eliminate the mistakes of the past in order to build a more successful future.

Lisa Su, CEO of Advanced Micro Devices (AMD) states, "I've always encouraged my teams to stay focused and determined to succeed in the face of significant challenges." Under Su's leadership, AMD stock value rose from $4 in 2014 to $75, a 1,700 percent increase. One can only attribute such a company turnaround to outstanding leadership. A mentor told Su to "run toward problems."

It's easy for a leader to express kind words, such as, "Things will get better," "It's OK," "Don't worry about it," or "Everything is great." It is a great leader's job to worry about the issues, not sugar coat the situation. Exceptional leaders master details in preparation for change. Great leaders accept reality as it is and take action.

A Leader Sets the Standards

> *When systems do fail, a leader should start fixing them*
> *by looking into a mirror.*
> —D. Michael Abrashoff

Whenever you are not getting the results that you want, instead of blaming someone else, ask yourself what ***you*** can do differently to get the desired results. It could be: (1) being clear about what is involved in getting the job done; (2) providing additional training; (3) giving people more time to work; or (4) adding resources.

A great team has standards of excellence that define what is and is not acceptable. When you allow your expectations to slip, your level of success will decrease alongside your team effort, work ethic, and sense of pride. It is your job as leader to maintain high standards.

CASE STUDY 11: THE SUDDENLY ABSENT

Kitty is new at her job in the dental office. She just made it past the ninety-day probationary period. She stated in her initial interview that she wanted to work Fridays, even though this is a nondoctor day. Her first Friday, she missed. The second Friday was a holiday. The third Friday, Kitty told the doctor before leaving on Thursday night that she would be there the next day. She left work healthy. The next morning Kitty called in sick. Kitty has now missed two work Fridays.

Solution:

Are you, as leader, going to have the courage to sit down with a new employee, to tell her that you see a pattern with her attendance, documenting a verbal warning that if attendance does not improve then the Friday work day will no longer be given to her?

This is an uncomfortable conversation. But if attendance concerns are not addressed head-on by you, the boss, it is likely that this pattern will continue. Best to discuss it immediately. Make it clear that absenteeism is noticed, undesirable, and being documented. After the meeting, no further Fridays were missed. Kitty turned out to be an excellent employee.

A LEADER LEADS BY EXAMPLE

I've searched all the parks in all the cities and found no statues of committees.
                                        –Gilbert K. Chesterton

A leader must be unyielding about the goal but flexible about the means. No job is too small or too unimportant for the leader. Everyone is watching and behaving accordingly. The signals that the leader send make all the difference.

As the leader, you will be dealing with capable and incapable staff. Hopefully, time taken in your working interviews before hiring will keep incapable employee situations to a minimum. **What great HR managers know is that not everyone has unlimited potential.** As a practice owner, you will constantly be evaluating performance and managing or weeding out as the reality of each situation dictates.

With competent team members, there is often no need to check work. The results are voluntarily achieved and presented. When dealing with the incompetent, you have three options: do the work yourself and hope that your leadership by example catches on; reassign this team member to another function; or encourage them to move on. Should this situation apply to a volunteer organization, such as a dental society, replacement may not be an option. You must just grin and bear dysfunction, and in some cases do the work of others.

Seek First to Understand

Behind every communication problem
is a sweaty ten-minute conversation
that you don't want to have.

–Gay Hendricks

As the leader, especially when dealing with HR issues, be the first to make a move toward behavioral improvement. By saying nothing, you will not prevent the problem from continuing to happen.

Let's consider some simple "first talk" wording. Try this:

"It seems like we're facing a challenge. My goal is to understand your perspective and to make sure that I hear you out regarding your issues so that we can work on solving them together for the benefit of our patients, our team, our office, and your employment."

Take notes during your discussion. Perhaps the solution will appear to the individual during the meeting. If not, kindly tell them that the next time it happens, you will need to write them up, and with further repetition, the undesirable behavior may lead to termination.

People are complex. So are the situations they create. Differences in experience, culture, or language can lead to misunderstanding the rules of employment. Be sure that your employees always know that meeting workplace expectations are central to fulfilling their crucial roles as front-line providers of dental health care.

A Leader Appreciates Diversity

I make it very clear that no one can claim
to be a better human being than another.
A dishwasher is as important in this organization
as a vice president.

–Horst Schulze

We all have unique backgrounds. Just having lived in three parts of the United States—Boston, Chicago, and San Francisco—I can tell you that the culture of each region is completely different.

No matter where you are from, recognize that we are all diverse but nonetheless have similarities that have great value. The context of communication is shaped by our own unique back stories. We make assumptions based on our unique situations. We each have our own lenses and filters. The intended meaning of the speaker and perceived meaning of the listener can be radically different. When exceptional encounter behavior that may appear to be unacceptable, they wonder what it is that they don't understand about the person or their communication processes.

In situations of diversity, a calm leader has the mindset that everyone has good intentions. Every person is doing their best to further the overall good of the organization. If trouble arises, it might be attributable to an easily correctable misunderstanding. Have the courage to ask what is not understood about a situation before jumping to a conclusion.

A Leader Avoids Negativity

Being positive won't guarantee you'll succeed.
But, being negative will guarantee you won't.

–Jon Gordon

As leader, in order to protect positivity, optimism, and focus, make a conscious decision to weigh the worth of any activity in which you are asked to participate. There will be times when you will need to ask yourself, "Is this experience a positive or a negative influence on my leadership, business success, and life?"

Some virtual online meetings during the pandemic were amazing. Some were negative gloom fests that devolved into drinking binges. Some online meetings shared knowledge. Others shared toxicity. Avoid negativity like the plague! Or, shall I say, avoid negativity like COVID!

As caring professionals, our job is to provide hope for better health. This includes psychological health. To be a leader, you must manage yourself first. Be the type of leader that you would want to follow by sticking with things that are positive, helpful, and hopeful.

A Leader Stays Optimistic

If you believe it will work out, you'll see opportunities.
If you believe it won't, you will see obstacles.

–Wayne Dyer

The leader sets the tone. Optimists expect a successful future. Optimists make more effort and are more persistent when they encounter obstacles. Optimists shrug off setbacks. Optimists make fantastic leaders.

When a leader imagines the future in a positive way, their demeanor will spill over onto their team. The leader's enthusiasm can't help but be contagious. This enables everyone on the team to act on building a successful future together.

We've all known a glass-half-full person who is the epitome of a high-morale optimist. They are nice to be around. Don't dismiss this person as a dreamer or a Pollyanna. An exceptional leader conceptualizes reality as the water present and not the glass. You need to start with how much water you have. Your glass can be full. You are just picturing the wrong size glass in your current situation. To avoid being a pessimist, accept your glass and be grateful for what you already have. Plan and build from that point on. Perhaps you can work to make your glass overflow!

In their book, *The Art of Possibility: Transforming Professional and Personal Life,* Roz and Benjamin Zander set forth an unemotional interpretation of accepting reality. They call this practice "Being the Board." Your board, such as one used in a board game like chess, hosts your situation as a game being played out. You are in charge of how you would like the game to be played. This allows you to manipulate the problematic conditions from the outside world to inside the boundaries of yourself and your board.

Blaming does nothing to solve your perceived problems. There is nothing you can do about others' actions or mistakes. You can only control your own actions. You are in charge of your response to whatever may happen. Your assumptions may be the source of your own difficulty. Understand that you are what you are today because of the choices that you made yesterday. Be careful but proactive in your decision-making process.

Encourage those with positive can-do attitudes to take the lead in your dental office. Help others to get on the optimism train. Leave the pessimists at the station.

A Leader Creates Other Leaders

> *Outstanding leaders go out of their way*
> *to boost the self-esteem of their personnel.*
> *If people believe in themselves, it's amazing*
> *what they can accomplish.*
>
> −Sam Walton

Your people are your business. Your frontline workers, including the financial coordinator, the receptionist, and the treatment coordinator, help to generate tens of thousands of dollars in business in your dental office just by being pleasant, upbeat, and taking great care of your patients. These are, without a doubt, the keystone of your team.

You may be surprised to realize that it isn't the doctor who most likely makes the first impression in your dental office; it is whoever answers the new-patient phone call. They must have the three "A's"—being Available, Affable, and Able. This person is an important leader in their own right, growing your business by doing his or her job with excellence.

Everyone on your team is a customer service leader building relationships with your patients. Make sure that each employee understands that it is their full-time job to make every patient always feel welcomed and important.

BE BOLD IN THE FACE OF POLITICS

Politics is when people choose their words and actions
based on how they want others to react
rather than based on what they really think.
–Patrick Lencioni

We've all seen them. The dentists who are at every organizational meeting. They are extremely well-dressed. They always have smiles on their faces. They work the room from person to person, shaking everyone's hand. They are there to see and be seen. They are there to know and be known. And they have made a special effort to seek out everyone on the next nomination committee. They're running for yet another office of yet another organization. They are "The Politicians."

This is perhaps the greatest ailment in volunteer organizations, the domination of leadership opportunities by a few career politicians. Behind the scenes, hard-working volunteers, those with years of service, are working to make the organization successful, thinking to themselves, "Can't someone else have a chance at leadership?"

What happens when politics overtake a volunteer organization? Overlooked hard-working people get demoralized. At that point they have two options: speak up or quit.

Men have patriarchal political networks spanning back hundreds of years in fraternal organizations such as social clubs and country clubs. Men co-nominate each other. Without access to these same networks, women are often overlooked for leadership positions, even though they add great value and make large contributions to the success of the organizations that they loyally serve.

Forget the women's march for equality. Support other women right where you are. If you are a woman in a man's organization, support yourself if no one else will. It's taken a long time for society to accept diversity. Now is the time to work on equity and inclusion.

Twelve Principles of Courageous Leadership

*When life seems hard, the courageous
do not lie down and accept defeat;
instead, they are all the more determined
to struggle for a better future.*
                                    –Queen Elizabeth II

In your personal efforts to be a courageous leader, you will be managing yourself. Take time to understand yourself, and your situation, as well as that of others. Have an open, inquisitive mind. A constant quest for knowledge brings about a greater understanding of any set of circumstances.

Be honest about your responsibility as leader. Set an example of courage for others to follow. Take advantage of the opportunity to change the present. Take a risk. Go first. Communicate what you have decided. Be bold.

Being the leader is a difficult job. Your productivity and results will be the legacy that you leave behind. The lion's share of what you receive during your leadership may be criticism, blame, and complaints. Be strong and be prepared for this eventuality. Your future is determined by what you believe and do. Actions speak louder than words. Do the right thing.

Here are a few final thoughts to help you on your difficult leadership journey.

1. *Stay strong; pressure strengthens you.*
2. *Prioritizing principles enhances your value over time.*
3. *Serve a purpose.*
4. *Ask yourself, "How can I give?"*
5. *Live with hope.*
6. *Work to fulfill a higher purpose and justice.*
7. *Surrender to the experience and be adaptable.*
8. *Everyone has freedom of choice.*
9. *Your future is determined by what you believe and do.*
10. *Give your organization unconditional love.*
11. *Do the right thing.*
12. *Remember leaders go last.*

There is only one true type of leadership: servant leadership. Your window of leadership opportunity will not last forever. "This too shall pass." Accomplish what you can, when you can. Stick with the courage of your convictions. Never give up.

PART TWO

TEAMWORK

The strength of the team is each individual member.
The strength of each member is the team.

–Phil Jackson

W e've all heard the adage, "Chains are only as strong as their weakest link." What is your team's weakest link? It could be a staff member's performance. It may be a weak leader. Or, it could be someone "rocking the boat" of progress through dysfunctional workplace behaviors.

The team can be burdened by one individual who does not follow through on the cultural standard. This could be due to an emotional issue, nonparticipation, or poor attendance. It could be lack of enthusiasm or negativity, which, rather than elevating the team, pulls the team down. Even a superstar who is an outstanding performer that can't share the stage with anyone else will diminish teamwork.

Whenever the weakest link is found, it will take courage, communication, and candor as well as time, energy, and attention to turn the weakest link into a stronger link.

On a dental team, it's one team, one score, and everyone counts. Your score is the result of everyone's contribution. As dental practice owners, we will be training, motivating, and co-elevating your team throughout your entire career. Removal of the link to benefit the strength of the chain is sometimes necessary. We will find ourselves continuously working to improve the weakest link on our own team and even within ourselves.

Chapter 9

CULTURE

Culture is not just one thing; it's everything.
—Jon Gordon

L ike wind, culture is invisible. Yet, it is felt. When I think of a positive culture, I think of a bright, sunshiny day. This happy work environment is comfortable for everyone to do their best work. We want patients and families to feel joy and love in our dental practices. In this way, culture is an ecosystem.

As leader of your dental practice, your goal is to have your team culture wind at your back, not blowing against you. Start by knowing what you want in terms of your standards. Then build your desired practice culture and maintain it.

You are in control of your office culture by what you allow and what you prohibit in your practice space. Cultural "good vibes" permeate every successful business. There will be a positive impact on your financial bottom line. A positive culture is a competitive advantage.

THREE COMPONENTS OF A WINNING CULTURE

In his book, *Culture Code: The Secrets of Highly Successful Groups,* author Daniel Coyle states that culture has three components:

1. *Safety—connection, belonging, and identity;*
2. *Vulnerability—mutual risk, trust, and cooperation; and*
3. *Purpose—live and communicate shared goals and values.*

Let's begin by defining your team culture. Once you decide what your desired team culture should be, you will know what needs to be preserved at all costs and what needs to be eliminated.

TWENTY-FIVE POSITIVE TRAITS OF A WINNING TEAM

A great team culture is not easy to build, and even harder to maintain. Start by asking your staff:

"What do we expect our winning team culture standard to be? What do we require of ourselves and our teammates? What do we want our positive team culture to feel like? How can we interact at work each day to make our best team culture possible?"

Here are the responses of my team to the Winning Team Culture Questionnaire.

Appreciative
Caring
Diverse
Educated
Energetic
Enthusiastic
Ethical
Experienced
Fun
Friendly
Generous
Hardworking
Inspirational
Kind
Loving

Meticulous
Outgoing
Professional
Positive
Polite
Reliable
Respectful
Safe
Social
Well-rounded

Now that we know what we want to be, we can hang these values on the wall as a continuous reminder of the qualities that we live and value. These are the sum of the positive behaviors of the people we have chosen to have on our team. Try this exercise with your own team and choose to begin creating your desired team culture.

TWENTY-ONE NOT TOLERATED TRAITS OF A WINNING TEAM

Firms must be intolerant on matters of values or strategy,
if these are to be sustained.
–David H. Maister

When I think of a negative, unacceptable team culture, I think of tension. Communication is poor. Stress is present. The climate is like a cloudy day. The environment is gloomy. It's that "walking on eggshells" feeling, and it just might start pouring rain at any moment. You're unsettled and cautious. You're guarded and can't bring your full self to work. It is an unsettled work environment.

In order to maintain your winning team culture, everyone must also know what will NOT be tolerated. Undesirable actions and attitudes cannot be allowed if you are to maintain a winning team culture of success.

Ask your team the almighty questions:

"What will we not tolerate on our winning team to maintain our positive team culture? What actions would cause us to eliminate a team member?"

Here are the responses of my staff regarding what we will not tolerate on our winning team:

Bad Attitude
Blaming Others
Brutality
Bullying
Drama
Incompetence
Lack of Time Management
Lateness
Laziness
Messiness
Negativity
Non-team Player
Poor Attendance
Poor Judgement
Rudeness
Selfishness
Unknowledgeable
Unprofessional
Unreliable
Untrustworthy
Wasteful

It's Not Morale, It's Attitude

The only disability in life is a bad attitude.
—Scott Hamilton

If you look at the Twenty-One Traits Not Tolerated list, probably all undesirable traits can be attributed to one source: a bad attitude. If every person on your team had a great attitude, one of gratefulness, passion, and motivation, low morale would not be able to exist.

Morale refers to an internal feeling, which depends on the overall environment. It is based on the satisfaction, and the outlook of the person in their work milieu. If someone is talking about poor morale, then it is a given that attitudes are less than ideal. If an individual is focused on negativity, they are feeding poison to their mind. Due to a bad attitude, and quite possibly to the attitudes of those around them, they will have low morale.

Business consultant Tom Peters states that the number-one killer of morale in the workplace is layoffs. I would state that morale is also diminished by financial hardship and social strife between team members. Negative conversations and depressed demeanors can also adversely affect positive feelings. Be aware of these factors and work to eliminate them from your office as quickly as possible.

A bad attitude is the number-one most intolerable work behavior. When you find a team member in a less than sunshiny mood, it is probably due to bad attitude, not low morale. *Low morale is the end result of the behaviors listed on the negative Traits Not Tolerated list.* Whatever it is that has diminished your winning team culture, it is most likely due to someone's bad attitude, which you, as leader, must identify and correct before it contagiously alters morale.

Work done with a bad attitude is like a desert storm pushing sand in your eyes. Taken to the extreme, negative attitudes result in a toxic workplace. Nip negativity and unwanted dysfunctional behaviors in the bud. Do not allow them to exist as part of your practice culture.

Three-hundred-sixty-degree reviews are a great way for the team to identify and to make suggestions for a positive attitude tune-up. Ask everyone on your team, "What does this team member do best?" and

"What can this person improve?" Gather, read, and review the answers individually with each employee. Call out negative behaviors for elimination to benefit the entire group.

You may find suggestions like, "You're not the only one who gets tired at 4:30 p.m.!" These negative comments can be turned around if the team member is made aware that their actions and demeanor affect others. When reviewing such behaviors, sandwich improvement recommendations between two positive comments to produce a win-win for everyone on the team.

Eliminate Negativity

> One of the biggest mistakes leaders make
> is that they ignore the negativity within
> their team and organization.
>
> –Jon Gordon

Left unattended, negative tendencies hurt success. **To have a well-run office, accept that practice culture cannot be a choice.** Practice culture is a standard of behavior to which every team member needs to conform as a requirement of employment. Undesirable actions must be addressed and changed immediately to ensure a highly functioning team. If your office cannot maintain a positive team culture, it will be impossible for you to develop a good reputation and a brand image of which you can be proud.

High standards, rigidly enforced, foster accomplishment, and build the prestige of any organization. *Where standards are high, the culture is strong.* A less-than-ideal culture can be due to laissez-faire leadership.

Most people want to work in an office with high standards applied fairly to create an ideal and fair work environment. I remember a time when I had an extremely negative person working in my practice. I would show up each day eager and optimistic, ready to cheerfully serve my patients and my team. Then along came Ms. Gloom, a low energy individual, with a downpour of complaints that exhausted everyone's passion. It was a difficult time. We were relieved when Ms. Gloom finally quit.

One of the hardest things you will ever handle as a leader is managing and eliminating this type of negativity. You cannot change a medical condition such as depression. You may not be able to affect someone's personal issues or personality traits. It will be your task as a leader to not hire an energy vampire in the first place, or swiftly act if presented with such a threat.

The first step in stopping unwanted behavior is to talk about it. You can start by having a private conversation with this person to let them know how their behavior upsets the team. Let the negative employee know that you will not allow them to sabotage your positive team culture. This intervention alone might save the day.

Be a positive force for change. You don't want to lose good team members because of an unpleasant person with whom no one wants to work. It is good to remember: if you want to work with people who smile, hire people who smile.

EIGHT CONDITIONS WHICH CHALLENGE A POSITIVE ATTITUDE

Here are threats to a positive work environment on which you can take immediate action.

1. *An uncomfortably hot office*
2. *Malfunctioning equipment*
3. *Misunderstandings*
4. *Poor communication*
5. *Quarreling*
6. *Termination*
7. *Financial difficulties*
8. *Unfair leadership*

Since the 1930s, when the Western Electric Hawthorne Works plant studied lighting on worker productivity, industrial psychologists have been aware of the effects of such environmental variables. Pay attention to your own environment. Plush surroundings are not necessary. The granite countertops might even be counterproductive. Comfort and lightness of mood are a must for high productivity and positive attitudes.

The wonderful thing about your office environment is that you can control the variables. You may want to make your environment physically bright but don't overlook the importance of human engineering, such as always being cheerful. Something as simple as saying, "Good morning," "Good night," or "Great to see you again" sets the tone for a happy team.

Take time to focus on housekeeping, safety, and equipment. No one wants to work in an unorganized office. Play pleasant music. Have an air freshener to keep your place of business smelling great. Offer bottled water. Keep the office temperature cool for an energetic team. Smiling and laughing will translate into a warm welcome at the front desk. Happy team members move with freedom. Being comfortable in all aspects of their work environment keeps your team feeling great.

Most people seek peace and harmony in their lives and at work. This includes being around people who are positive, make good choices, and have an upbeat demeanor.

Emotional intelligence applies to both the leader and the employees. Outbursts are unacceptable behavior in a professional setting. To help prevent unwanted situations, it is helpful for the owner and the team to talk about what triggers them and what positive cues they need to do their best work.

FIVE STEPS FOR DEALING WITH FAILURE

There is no failure except in no longer trying.
–Elbert Hubbard

When adversity strikes, deal with it promptly and the disappointment will soon dissipate. Here are five steps to deal with failure:

1. *Gather your team.*
2. *Take a moment to whine.*
3. *Research what happened, accept it, and do not take it personally.*

4. *Create a solution to prevent this problem from ever happening again.*
5. *Improve from the failure and move on.*

We will all fail. After falling, what matters is that you get back up. Diagnose, treat, and resolve to avoid shortcomings in the future.

You may have had a team member failure. The performance or personality of one person may not have worked out. Perhaps they lacked common sense, were untrainable, or had a personality disorder. What are your choices? You can reassign the person if they have other talents. We can call this, "The Peter Principle of Reassigned." The second option is that the troublesome employee be removed or encouraged to resign.

It is OK to whine about failure as you brainstorm to find a solution. Despite your total commitment to your practice, things will not always be perfect. Not every patient or staff member will be ideal. You will encounter pitfalls. Allow some complaining when issues arise, but keep focused on solutions so that problems never happen again. Discuss these situations with your team and be open to learning from them. This receptivity will encourage office communication. It will also make your office a safer space.

Limited whining will give you and your team emotional relief. You will have the satisfaction of knowing that you worked together to do the best you could. Such chances to exhale are an important element of failure, vulnerability, and building trust. I'm sure that Thomas Edison whined about a few of his ten thousand failed light bulb experiments! Once you have vented, gather the rubble and press on to success.

Focus on How Things Are

The data sets us free.
–James P. Lewis

Do not be afraid to say, "I believe we can do better." However, how you want things to be is not reality. Focus on how things actually are now. It will always take courage to call attention to areas which need improvement.

"Should be" is not action. Beware of "If, And, or But" responses. Be alert for statements that start with "If only..." or "But, Doctor..." Remember that, "If ands or buts were candy and nuts, every day would be Christmas Eve!" Do not accept excuses or play the blame game.

Placing blame does nothing to change a situation. *Focus on, state, and take action on what needs to be done to accomplish the results you are seeking.* Remember, data is unemotional and objective. Check into your own practice management software reports. Which aspects could help you elevate your team and your daily team score?

There is no guessing when data is presented. At your team meeting, or business plan review (BPR), everyone looks at one set of numerical facts. Talk about data with candor and respect. The data sets us free from speculation, guessing, and needless anxiety. When in doubt, get more data.

Dashboards, figures, pie charts, and graphs can make the difference between a good company and a great company. Measurement brings focus to specific areas needing attention. Numbers are the language of business that expresses progress. Measuring enables improvement.

An example: You can readily measure how many new patients were successfully scheduled to start treatment each month. If your number is deemed not high enough, you need to make more phone calls, send more postcards, or do more marketing. Verbal responses or excuses ("But, Doctor...") to performance queries do not equate with hard metrics. Do not rely upon what someone thinks about the work being done. Actual data about what is happening in your practice or deposited into your practice checking account is what matters.

MOTIVATION

Put me in, Coach!

–Jeffrey Gitomer

Do you leave a team meeting feeling energized? One of your team goals must be to motivate and co-elevate each other, giving an extra push to reach your goals.

I will never forget hearing teamwork legend Coach K at an AAO Annual Session as keynote speaker. Mike Krzyzewski led two Olympic gold medal basketball teams as well as Duke. He spoke about inspirational rituals and the visualization of success. His most moving story was about a Duke player who cried out from the bench, "Let's GO!" when the team was down. At that very moment, the game turned around. That battle cry was all it took to add motivation, changing a losing game into a victory.

It's the same with your dental team. When things get complacent, give out a cry, "Let's GO!" Who doesn't love basketball? Shouldn't your dental team feel as excited about their own score? Level A players want to be in the game. They want to win!

I recently hired two new dental assistants. They were eager and excited to learn. Their enthusiasm was refreshing. I am amazed how quickly they picked up the requirements of the job and how well they served the patients. Jolene, my lead RDA of twenty-five years, coached these new assistants. She has trained over forty dental assistants. This is her legacy. Even now in retirement, she still comes back to train; she is still saying, "Put me in!"

You can't just go through the motions while working in a dental office. Your head has got to be in the game. We can't hire people who watch the clock for lunch or for the day to end. I have a rule in my office: don't discuss lunchtime in front of patients. We have ninety minutes scheduled for our lunch break every day. That's more than enough time and well past the half-hour minimum required by law in the state of California. While the patient is seated in the chair, I want all attention on the patient, not how many more minutes until lunch.

No matter what else is going on, while in the dental office, an employee's thoughts need to be about the patient. Internal personal distractions need to be turned off while working in a dental office. Negative emotions cannot be allowed to drive poor customer service. Everyone needs to always have their head in the game!

Vision

*If you are working on something you really care about,
you don't need to be pushed. The vision pulls you.*

–Steve Jobs

Refocus your team by continuing to share the vision—over and over again—the big picture of what you are trying to accomplish, what your office stands for, and your "WHY." The vision is bigger than any individual.

If you're going to be the number-one office in your area, share your HOW. Remind your team what your vision statement means to you. Every day, we have the opportunity to improve someone's life through dentistry. This is meaningful work. This is how we contribute to a better world.

Smiles change lives

As an exercise, have your employees recite your vision. Ask each team member at the next meeting to say what specifically the vision means to them. People who lose the big picture, thinking about themselves and their own personal woes and failures, give up. It's always about the vision. In the dental office, it's always about serving the patient.

When I think of our vision, *Smiles change lives,* I think of the retrognathic kindergartener who came to my orthodontic office with his parents after trying to kill himself by running out into the street the first day of school. Kids called him "Bucky Beaver." We changed his life by performing an osseous distraction, lengthening his lower jaw with orthodontic treatment, giving him confidence, comfort, and a beautiful smile.

I think of a sad single woman with a disfiguring protrusion and open bite, long face syndrome, and gummy smile that we beautified through orthodontic treatment including bicuspid extraction, and orthognathic surgery including a maxillary impaction. She soon after got married and became a successful business woman.

I think of the young woman with a canted occlusal plane and off-centered maxillary midline who looked sad, asking for help. Here transformation through orthodontic treatment, periodontal recontouring, and restorative treatment built her confidence and improved her social life. She soon got married and transitioned to a new career.

For the vision to come alive, it must mean something concrete and real to each individual. When people know how they contribute to a vision bigger than themselves, they have a purpose. Motivation soars.

MISSION

Caring professionals serving valued patients

Are you living your mission? Do you even know your mission? Peter Drucker said, "A mission statement should fit on the back of a t-shirt." Keep it short so you can remember it, recite it, and live it. Ask each team member to quote your mission statement now, and each year at your annual reviews.

CORE VALUES

Clinical excellence
Outstanding customer service
A great patient experience

If I say, "Tell me about your office," is everyone on your team going to tell me something different? Your core values are your staff's elevator pitch when someone asks about your practice. Will what they tell me inspire me to go to your office?

Your core values outline your strategy. If you are a united team, you and your team share and live your core values.

TAGLINE

Your smile is our inspiration

Put together your own tagline. Print these aspirations in your Team Handbook and on your marketing ephemera. Keep your branding top-of-mind.

Mantra

One team, one score

The mantra of the Three Musketeers was, "One for All, and All for One." You too need a mantra to unite your team. When faced with difficult situations, fall back on these words. This phrase will propel your team's performance and culture.

Teamwork as a Competitive Advantage

As a leader or an employer, your biggest responsibility is to coach and encourage your people to succeed. Coach them to be excellent. Coach them to score. Coach them to win.
—Jeffrey Gitomer

Do you reward the team or the individual? When the team wins, everyone wins. You reward the team. I'm not saying that you don't have a high scorer. The Chicago Bulls were better with Michael Jordan than without him. But Michael Jordan could not have played basketball alone. He needed someone to pass him the ball to score. He needed his team. So it is with you and your dental team.

If you have a bonus system and you reach your goal, everyone on the team gets a bonus, including the doctor. Should individual recognition be given for outstanding achievement, such as a most valuable player, it should be provided with respect to what this person contributed to the team.

I heard an orthodontist once state that if the office does well, he gives a bonus to the treatment coordinator. What about everyone else on the team? A team member answered the phone, took the records, helped the doctor to place the braces, cleaned the instruments, and put in extra effort staying late for a same-day start. Everyone on the team worked together. Everyone deserves a reward and recognition. If your number-one value is teamwork, recognize teamwork. In the long run, teamwork pays off for everyone.

Chapter 10

TRUST

Remember, teamwork begins by building trust
and the only way to do that is to
overcome our need for invulnerability.
                                        –Patrick Lencioni

T rust is built over time. But I once had a team member where this was not the case. Something was not quite right. This one person on my staff had a problem fitting in. She treated me well and communicated with me well, but she was not a team player. She did not offer help to her teammates. She didn't want to join team functions. When it came time to leave for the day, all that her teammates saw was her back as she walked out the door.

Early in my career, I didn't realize how important a friendly hello was for the start of a good day. This small gesture sets a tone of teamwork. I also didn't realize how important it was to ask each person if they needed help before leaving the office for the day. Saying goodbye to each of your teammates is a sign that you care about them and look forward to working together again.

It happened that I joined my husband for an overseas trip. It was a long flight, so I needed a good book to read on the journey. In the airport bookstore, I came across *The Five Dysfunctions of a Team: A Leadership Fable,* by Patrick Lencioni. At first, the title scared me. It was as if I did not want to know that I had a dysfunctional team member. Bravely, I picked up the book and purchased it. On the plane, I started reading. It changed my practice life forever. What I learned was that vulnerability and trust are the very foundation of teamwork that I was able to establish to this day.

THE SIX PILLARS OF TEAMWORK

> *Nobody cares how much you know until*
> *they know how much you care.*
> –Theodore Roosevelt

My team and I codified our basic building blocks of teamwork—The Six Pillars of Teamwork, into the following acronym:

TO CARE.
Trust,
  Ownership,
    Communication,
      Accountability,
        Results, and
          Excellence.

One basic requirement on a great team is that you must care about your patients and team success more than your personal, immediate wants and needs. Let's review each element of TO CARE one by one.

TRUST

> *He who does not trust enough will not be trusted.*
> –Lao Tzu

Trust is the essential basis of all good relationships. In the dental office, in organizations, and especially in a family, you must trust those who surround you. You must trust that team members will do what is best for the patients, the team, and the office. Finally, your patients must trust that you will take great care of them.

TEAM TRUST

> *Without trust, we don't truly collaborate;*
> *we merely coordinate or, at best, cooperate.*
> *It is trust that transforms a group of people into a team.*
> —Stephen M. Covey

In the back of Patrick Lencioni's classic book, *The Five Dysfunctions of a Team,* is a Team Assessment Test. It serves as a diagnostic tool to determine your staff's susceptibility to the five dysfunctions of teamwork: Absence of trust, fear of conflict, lack of commitment, avoidance of accountability, and inattention to results. Years ago, my team and I took the test. One team member was deficient in the area of trust. We took the next step in developing trust, answering short personal questions, including the vulnerability questions: "What were your unique challenges of childhood, your first job, and your worst job?"

The "lack of teamwork" team member could not answer these questions. When asked, she stood up and went to the coffee maker. Anything to avoid answering these questions. When she finally did answer them, her curt answer was, "Never had a worst job." End of conversation.

She was hiding something. Avoiding some deep pain. As the years passed, we found out more. She had been placed on probation as a minor. She was a single mom. She had arguments with her parents. She had a difficult life. Trusting others was not her forte. She eventually moved on to a corporate job. She taught us all what lack of vulnerability and strained teamwork felt like. It was caused by an absence of trust.

When you open up to your team members, you feel their struggle. But your office need not be a rehabilitation center. This is where dentists suffer at their own peril. Often with HR issues, dentists are too nice. Allowing lack of trust situations to persist leaves the team with the feeling of "walking on eggshells." It creates the need for "snoopervision" by the owner. If there are small infractions of trust, it leads to bigger problems.

Trust is a valuable team trait that builds confidence that no one is alone in the efforts to make the practice a success. You can trust that your teammates are there to help. Trusting relationships reinforce a web of reciprocal belief in one another.

Doctor Trust

> *The best way to find out if you can trust*
> *somebody is to trust them.*
> –Ernest Hemingway

Trust works in two directions. You can't expect your team to trust you if you don't trust them. Trust grows with dependability of actions. The doctor is trusted to make the practice a success. The same goes for the team members. Trust is built through actions and everyone's demonstrable ongoing ability to consistently work together.

The owner/doctor must be totally dedicated and proud of being trustworthy. Open-book management is a key transparency and trust-building move. It gives the message, "Here is the data. There is nothing to hide." It's one team, one score. Open-book management is a dynamic for everyone on the team. The team needs to know what the score is at all times if they are to care about it.

Patient Trust

Trust extends to and from our patients. Patients trust us to do the very best treatment possible. We trust that they are going to be compliant with care, and that they will pay us. We trust that our patients are going to follow through with the treatment and payment plans. If a patient continues to pose problems for your office, then perhaps it is best that they get "a fresh start" somewhere else. Mutual trust is the bedrock of an ideal doctor-patient relationship.

OWNERSHIP

Show me an organization in which employees take ownership,
and I'll show you one that beats its competitors.
–D. Michael Abrashoff

You see it, you own it. This is the mantra of ownership. Don't pass the buck to someone else. There is no "team" in ownership. There is only one owner of your responsibilities—you. Don't leave action items unattended. Open your mind, use your imagination, and find better ways of doing things. Be the solution, not the problem.

Ownership can have several meanings from the most minute detail to the big picture of the organization. For ownership team building, I love The Immersion Exercise of Dr. Thomas D. Zweifel, author of the book *Strategy-In-Action: Marrying Planning, People and Performance*. It goes like this:

Ask the team to reflect on your company's history. List key milestones. Tape four flip chart pages in a row. Give each team member slips of vertically narrow paper. Put the year on the left and have each team member write their milestone on the right. Have each team member initial their milestone. Start with the most distant date and have each team member discuss their milestone as they put it on the chart. New events can be added throughout the discussion. This exercise can take one to several hours. Your team ownership and loyalty will be strengthened through this exercise.

COMMUNICATION

No matter how much success you're having,
you can't continue working together if you can't communicate.
–Matt Cameron

The team is assembled for mandatory dental CPR training. We are all learning how to use the defibrillator. When the button is pressed, the defibrillator we are using does not actually work. Why? Because defibrillators are dangerous. This is why, after putting the pad leads on the chest of the patient, it is necessary to communicate, "Get back!"

What could happen if you are touching the victim or, even worse, touching the victim while kneeling in a pool of water and a defibrillator is activated? You could die. Yes, there are times when, if you do not communicate well, you could die.

The same holds true for US Navy SEALs. When under attack, the US Navy SEALs cannot be afraid to tell the leader what they need to do to stay safe or to keep the team safe. If the enemy is going to shoot the leader while he stands openly in a window, the team of SEALs needs to be able shout, "Get back!" Communicate with your leader, the team, and each other, as if life or death depends on it.

Dental teams need to have the doctor's back. Similarly, the leader has the backs of their staff members. Communication is bi-directional between team and leader. Communication must be truthful, immediate, strong, and open. This forthright style of communication is called candor.

Excellent communication can handle anything. The same holds true for your society or dental organization. You need to be able to say, "Hey, we're going to lose a lot of money if we do this," or, "This is a bad contract that needs to be renegotiated," or, "If we maintain this level of frivolous spending, we'll be bankrupt in four years!"

So, talk away, together and often! It mustn't be a therapy session, but open and honest dialog. Face-to-face, in-person communication in a group is always best. The team that communicates together, wins together.

THREE COMMUNICATION GUIDELINES

To facilitate team communication, here are three guidelines:

1. *Look each other in the eye.*
2. *Always tell the truth.*
3. *Don't interrupt the speaker.*

You have probably heard of the Native American talking stick. If the conversation gets out of control, you can always bring out the talking stick. The person with the talking stick has everyone's attention. In parliamentarian terms, the speaker has the floor! "Don't interrupt the speaker" is perhaps the hardest guideline to achieve.

If speech is occurring, but listening is not, you are still in trouble. There is no communication without listening. Listening is fifty percent of the communication equation. Great verbal skills can accomplish only so much. But great listening can produce breakthroughs and fulfilled employees.

Poor listening has adverse effects. Potential leaders leave. Isolation and fragmentation grow. There may be conflict. Trust might be so low as to engender a lawsuit. Taking time to communicate well, speaking openly, and listening well are the only sure ways to build a culture of trust.

ACCOUNTABILITY

To hold someone accountable is to care about them enough
to risk having them blame you for pointing
out their deficiencies.

–Patrick Lencioni

Accountability starts with personal commitment. Accountability is assured when a due date is placed on projects. You can't complete what you can't envision. Put in writing what you would like to achieve.

You can be an accountability superhero when you outline problems that need to be addressed. Then accept/assign responsibility for tackling it. To reach this mutual goal, use accountability language, such as, *"We are accountable for …"* or, *"We can meet this deadline."* Once trust in everyone's competence and capability is established, it's time to roll up your sleeves and let the work begin.

Results

> *I've always believed if you put in the work,*
> *the results will come.*
>
> –Michael Jordon

Results are your team score. When the numbers fall short of your goal, make the necessary adjustments. When your numbers are great, take time to celebrate your win. Never change a successful game plan.

Numbers are the language of business. Share your metrics. Motivation is the outcome of open-book management.

Excellence

> *Perfection is not attainable.*
> *But if we chase perfection, we can catch excellence.*
>
> –Vince Lombardi

You and your team are partners in the journey of, "Building the best dental practice possible." Clinical excellence and the success of your patient experience are your ultimate end game. Service excellence will be rewarded by growth of your reputation and business.

You have to pursue excellence individually as a dentist, while also shepherding a collective pursuit of excellence as a team. One important aspect of seeking excellence is surrounding yourself with others who have high personal standards. A rising tide raises all boats, even when you are not yet at high tide.

Excellence has many rewards. Let's review the ten benefits of excellence in the dental office with your team.

Ten Benefits of Excellence

1. *A high-quality dental service*
2. *Ability to delegate with confidence, resulting in a self-led team*
3. *Fewer write-offs*

4. *Great patient acceptance and conversion rate*
5. *Higher fees, greater earning power*
6. *High-caliber recruits and teammates*
7. *Lower team turnover*
8. *Greater morale, enthusiasm, productivity, and efficiency*
9. *Better customer reviews and brand marketing*
10. *Happier patients, team, doctor*

TEAM DIVERSITY

> *To effectively communicate,*
> *we must realize that we are all different in the way*
> *we perceive the world*
> *and use this understanding as a guide to our*
> *communication with others.*
> –Tony Robbins

In his book, *The 7 Habits of Highly Effective People,* Stephen R. Covey invites his readers to have an intellectual and emotional experience. He provides a line drawing and asks, "What do you see?" I showed the picture to my own team. They responded, "We see a young woman." I stated, "What if I told you this is a drawing of an old woman?" Who's right?

I showed my team the second picture where some lines of the same drawing were filled in black. "Now what do you see?" My team replied, "We still see a very elegant young woman." "What if I told you this is an old woman in her seventies?" Who's right?

I then showed my team the last picture. Now the drawing had crooked lines with white spaces. Now, everyone could clearly see the old woman. We had what might be called an "Aha!" moment. We understood that, "We see the world, not as it is, but as we are or, as we are conditioned to see it."

When we try to put into words what we see, we in effect describe ourselves, our perceptions, our paradigms. We assumed that we saw a young woman at first but then we got more information. This exercise is one that Stephen R. Covey did himself as a student at the Harvard Business School.

All team activities are valuable. Part of the bonding process which builds trust is simply expressing ourselves and spending time together, such as with team exercises.

At one meeting, I asked my team, "If you could play in a symphony orchestra, what instrument would you play?" One person answered, "the violin," another, "the triangle," another "the piano." I answered, "the flute." My financial coordinator answered, "I'd be the conductor!"

Wow! Conductor was the answer of leadership! This answer was naturally inherent to my financial coordinator, Lyndsay, a natural-born leader. She is outspoken and energetic; always goes first, candid, and she loves to lead. I came to a new understanding of her nature that day, which has helped me understand her better. This answer helped us to accept her innate tendency to lead. All that we need to do is get out of her way!

DISC

Personalities are comprised of four basic types—DISC: dominant, inspiring, supportive, and cautious. These personalities, which may be assessed either before or after hire, can be matched to the perfect job for that person. Personality profiling can help you better understand job applicants as well as the existing team.

Dominant

Direct, demanding, decisive, determined, doer. The dominant personality is a natural-born leader. The driver is outgoing, candid, decisive, and pragmatic. They make decisions quickly and are not timid about directing others. They enjoy it. They can even be a bit "bossy."

Dominant personalities are independent and efficient. They will not need much work direction. Tell them once, and consider it done. The dominant personality is perfect for the role of office manager or financial coordinator. Or a dominant person could be the doctor or leader. They will not be intimidated or derailed by any challenge.

But dominant individuals do not like to be controlled or, heaven forbid, "micromanaged." They thrive on their own independence and accomplishments. Under the right circumstances, the doctor and the office manager may both be co-dominant. For the benefit of the team, it is important that they both understand the nature of their personalities and leadership styles and lead together in harmony, without clashing.

INSPIRING

Influencing, interactive, impressive, involved. The inspiring personality is enthusiastic, spontaneous, persuasive, and capable of making an impression. They love people and don't mind saying so. They enjoy being with others and helping others. The inspiring influencer places emphasis on relationships. They are the office cheerleader.

The inspiring personality may be creative. They may wear colorful earrings, scarves, or wild-patterned shoes. This is all part of the fun they love to impart. They are likeable and empathetic. They connect quickly. This personality type is perfect for the dental office role of treatment coordinator.

SUPPORTIVE

Stable, steady, sweet, status quo, shy. The supportive personality is amiable and cooperative. They are loyal and reserved. They are considerate and diplomatic. This amiable personality is gentle, quiet, and kind.

The supportive personality places emphasis on cooperation, sincerity, and dependability. This personality is perfect for a quiet job such as a dental assistant or hygienist. They would make an ideal records manager, last-out receptionist, or insurance coordinator.

CAUTIOUS

Calculating, competent, conscientious, contemplative, careful. The analytical personality is precise, serious, and systematic. They place emphasis on quality, accuracy, expertise, and capability. They are task-oriented. They are prudent in their decisions and exhibit tremendous self-control. They are logical. All decisions are planned and well-thought-out.

The cautious personality is perfect for the roles of inventory or financial coordinator. With an analytical person in this role, your office will always be well-stocked and computer entries accurate. This individual also does well as payroll coordinator or HR manager. Their organizational skills and consistency will ensure that all is done correctly, by the policies and procedures of the office and laws of the state.

The DISC personality test is a valuable tool to help leaders and managers understand each team member's strengths. The DISC assessment can provide information for better selection and placement of new team members. It can also help in the selection process for a specific office function.

FIVE ACTIONS OF UNITY TRAINING

People who understand one another work better together.
–John C. Maxwell

Diversity, equity, inclusion, and belonging (DEIB). As a country, and in the dental profession, we have made great advances in terms of diversity. What we have not yet achieved is equity, inclusion, and belonging. Although we are all different, **teamwork is about unity training not diversity training.** Our goal is to have a unified team treated fairly and equitably, working together while feeling included and belonging. The goal of leadership is to have an aligned team working in harmony. Inclusion means that all feel welcome to join; belonging means that all feel comfortable staying. Individuals promoting themselves or members of their small clique at the exclusion of others is unacceptable. Yet this is what still happens in some offices and dental organizations.

By speaking up, we begin to turn the tides on equity, inclusion, and belonging. In your unity training, concentrate on people's like-mindedness, common aims, and core values, rather than their differences. Include everyone rather than treating some as VIPs. Treat men and women equally. Maximize uniqueness and contributions toward shared goals.

One threat to reaching unity on the DEIB front is microaggressions. I commend Dr. Nehi Ogbevoen on his article "What Are Microaggressions and How Do They Affect Us?" in the PCSO Bulletin, Summer of 2022. Dr. Ogbevoen explains that microaggressions occur in three forms: (1) microinsults; (2) microassaults; and (3) microinvalidations. Let's look closer into these categories.

1. Microaggressions
   Name calling, avoidant behavior, and purposeful discrimination. Non-verbal microaggressions include eyerolling and non-inclusion.
2. Microassaults
   Attempts to discredit or minimize the experiences of a person. Racial and sexist profiling.
3. Microinvalidations
   Rude and insensitive comments; assuming someone isn't smart or implying lack of morals. An example would be when one shares a time when they were disrespected and are interrupted by an opinion they were not discriminated against. Microinvalidations are often unconscious verbal and behavioral actions that exclude, negate, or nullify the thoughts, feelings, and experiences of an individual or group. A microinvalidation also includes asserting that a person's marginalized identity plays only a minor role in their life.

In his PCSO article, Dr. Ogbeveon writes that it is critical to continue to educate ourselves and to take steps to help create a more just world. Five actions that we can take to help make our offices, homes, communities, and dental societies more welcoming include:

1. *Educate ourselves and our teams about microaggressions.*
2. *Lead by example and address occurrences of microaggressions by calling them out appropriately.*
3. *Engage in difficult but crucial and authentic conversations and acknowledge that diverse personal experiences shape how we experience the world around us.*
4. *Own our personal intentions but understand that the impact on others matters.*
5. *Remember that microaggressions are cumulative and not just one single event.*

A microaggression is a subtle, perhaps unintentional, form of prejudice. Rather than an overt declaration of sexism, or racism, a microaggression often takes the shape of jokes, offhand comments, or pointed insults and actions. Microaggressions have been referred to as "death by a thousand little cuts" because constant slights can be devasting to our mental health. Microaggressions can even lead to post-traumatic stress disorder.

When you courageously address someone about a microaggression, try,

> "I am really curious and want to better understand why you said/did what you said/did," or,

> "I am not sure if you're aware, but this is how I'm receiving what was said/done. Was that your intention?"

If you've had a conversation and nothing has changed, at that point you're dealing with a microassault. If your dental society has a DEI Task Force or Ethics Committee, bring the situation to their attention, and ask for remediation of the situation.

FAIRNESS

> *Inclusion and fairness in the workplace . . .*
> *is not simply the right thing to do; it's the smart thing to do.*
> –Alexis Herman

When I think of total fairness, I think of symphony orchestra auditions behind a screen. Only the performance is evaluated, without looking at the identity of the individual. It was not until flutist Doriot Anthony Dwyer had an audition behind a screen for the Boston Symphony that she was accepted as the first woman member of a major symphony orchestra. I wish all of life could be like this type of audition or a standardized test. This is true meritocracy. No one can see who is playing the instrument or taking the test. All are treated equally.

If fair, there are no favorites on the dental team or in a dental society. If one employee has a review, everyone gets one. If one person gets a raise, everyone on the team gets a raise (including the doctor). There are no discriminatory practices or reactionary decisions. The policies and procedures as outlined in the Team Handbook apply equally to everyone.

There is no such thing as a truly level playing field in life, but it is important to work hard as an office or dental organization to make your environments as fair and as equitable as possible. **Fairness is a pillar of ethics.** For one team, one score, there are no favorites; in dental organizations, there should be no VIPs, just one team working together for the betterment of all.

Chapter 11

DISCIPLINE

Effective leadership is putting first things first.
Effective management is a discipline, carrying it out.

–Stephen R. Covey

H ow are you going to keep your positive team spirit in the midst of
bad news and negativity? As the leader of my team during the pandemic of 2020, to keep the energy of my team high, we started reading
US Navy SEAL books. Our absolute favorite was *Elite: High Performance
Lessons and Habits from a Former Navy SEAL* by Nick Hays. The deeper
that we dove, the more that we learned about grit. We were each trans-
formed from victimhood to a winning warrior mentality. Our studies
shaped us into a high-performance team.

THIRTEEN HIGH-PERFORMANCE LESSONS OF
US NAVY SEALs

Let's look at some SEAL ideals. Perhaps these concepts will help transform your office into a unit characterized by high coordination and
function.

1. *Take control of your thoughts.*

> *What we think, we become.*
> –Buddha

Your mind should be like social media. Swipe right to "like" and left to "block." Banish negative thoughts. Your thought process will lead to your reality. Visualize success and then work toward it.

Thinking of my own life, I always had positive thoughts that I would become an orthodontist. Since seventh grade, the thought of being anything else was unimaginable. I always wanted to marry a man from Harvard. Don't ask me why. It might have been because my mother took me to see the movie *Love Story,* where Ryan O'Neil is a Harvard student. In the movie, Ali McGraw attends Radcliffe (in real life, she graduated from Wellesley College, just like me!). Later, living in California, I met my husband in the San Francisco Harvard Club. He was listed in the directory, HMS '89. I was HSDM, '88. I sent him an email: "Hey, do I know you?" He asked me out on a blind date. The rest is history. He also needed orthodontic treatment. Strange coincidences. My high school year book reads that I wanted to marry a man from Harvard and be an orthodontist. My dreams came true!

What you put in your mind, sticks. If you can dream it, you can do it. Take control of your thoughts for your best reality. My dad used to say, "You have a choice every morning to be either happy or sad. You choose." Believing is seeing. The opportunities we seek and think in our mind will present themselves. We want to seize these moments. Think about what you could do right now to get you where you would like to be.

2. *Be mentally tough.*

High-performance individuals push past the negative comments, naysayers, bullies, pain, setbacks, and failures, and instead stay focused on their plan. Being mentally tough is perhaps the number-one trait of a highly functioning group.

Life will always have challenges. I remember several—the AIDS epidemic, the mortgage and loan crisis of the 1990s, the 9/11 attacks, the mortgage meltdown of 2008, the recession of 2011, wildfires, earthquakes, the COVID-19 pandemic, and personal setbacks—there will always be something to deal with. Continue on without fear. Accept what you must. Work on solutions and adapt. Remember always, "This too shall pass."

3. CHOOSE THE WARRIOR MENTALITY.

Will you be a victim or will you be a warrior?
–Nick Hays

On the first day of class at the Harvard School of Dental Medicine, the professor started by saying, "What you have done before doesn't matter now. What matters now is what you do here." The US Navy SEALs have a saying: "You earn your trident every day." An old Eastern Airlines commercial had a pilot delivering their tagline: "We earn our wings every day."

It's true for everyone. Nothing stays the same. There is no cruise control in life. Every single one of your decisions is either leading you to growth or decline. You need to make a conscious commitment to keep moving forward, to meet challenges head-on, as a life warrior.

4. ELIMINATE EXCUSES.

Mozart was out on the town on October 28, 1787, the night before his *Don Giovanni* opera premiere. At around midnight, Mozart went to his room and composed the overture to this brilliant work for the next day's performance. It's never too late! This is why I never mind getting reports at the very last minute. What you get right before the deadline just might be brilliant!

Have you ever had a team member who, when you ask about a project, will respond only with excuses? The major cop-out is: "Don't micromanage me!" Watch out for this defensive behavior. This person may be struggling from low performance. They need to blame something or someone else, anyone but themselves for the job not being done.

A little stress and guidance can help an excuse-maker. There's no "passing the buck" on a high-performance team. Point out their excuse and tell them to take action instead. Excuses deflect the stress needed to get real work done. Successful individuals embrace fear, worry, and stress, and press on. Adversity builds strength. Failure is much scarier than deadlines!

5. *SURROUND YOURSELF WITH THE RIGHT PEOPLE.*

> *Surround yourself with people that push you to do better.*
> *No drama or mess. Just higher goals and higher vibrations.*
> *Good times and positive energy. No jealousy. No hate.*
> *Simply bringing out the absolute best in each other.*
> —Warren Buffet

I have a best friend that I've had since college. I've known her for more than forty years. She is a critical thinker and brutally honest, seeing every side of a situation. I call her often and ask for her advice about how to deal with difficult situations. I know that she has my back and best interests at heart. Other than my husband and my sister, I trust her more than anyone else.

We all need people on our side for those times when we meet people who are *not* on our side. Distance yourself from negative energy vampires! It may be a fellow dentist, someone on your board, or an employee of an auxiliary dental business. There is nothing you can do about this person other than avoid them. It's no reflection on you. Remember, Jesus had Judas. The problem lies within them.

Surround yourself with people who share your level of commitment and passion. Encircle yourself with the right people and leverage an environment of trust. This applies to the culture of your practice. Look for people with whom you can share everything in your life, the good and the bad. This is your tribe. Many years later, these people will still be your trusted friends.

Just as you tell your team, "I believe in you," you, yourself, as a leader, will need people in your life who have faith in your aspirations. Be deliberate about who you hang out with. After assembling the right cadre of colleagues and friends, humble yourself. It will sting a bit to receive constructive and honest feedback, but you don't need to always be right. You want to be better. Accept honest, constructive criticism with humility.

6. GUARD YOUR TIME.

> *Treasure this day, and treasure yourself.*
> *Truly, neither will ever happen again.*
> —Ray Bradbury

Have your front desk receptionist guard your doctor time. Don't have every phone call put through. Don't schedule every rep who offers to buy you lunch. Protect your team's time as well.

Why are we so eager to give away what we have so little of and cannot get more of? And what is most precious of all? Time with our families. Should you be more concerned, then, by people taking your money or your time? When you are spending your time, you're spending your life. You can always get more money, but you cannot get more time.

How much time per day do you spend on your cell phone? Should social media take your time? Every minute that I spend with my husband and son is time that I will never regret. I wish I would have spent more time with my parents. They are gone now. I wish I could spend more time with my sister. She lives far away. When was the last time you called someone that you care about? What if they were no longer there?

Find your purpose and spend time on that. As I sit here writing this book at the San Francisco Conservatory of Music, I am spending time with my son, a violinist. Music lessons have made us spend more time together. Our son's music has taken us on family trips to the Intermountain Strings Institute in Salt Lake City, Utah; the Philadelphia International Music Festival in Bryn Mawr, Pennsylvania; the Boston University Tanglewood Institute in Lenox, Massachusetts; the Juilliard Summer Performing Arts Program in Geneva, Switzerland; and the Meadowmount School of Music in Westport, New York. All of these adventures have filled our hearts with joy and a common purpose as we support our son and spend quality time together. It has even given my work more meaning and helped me to have the solitude to write my books. This summer, we toured with the Young People's Symphony Orchestra in Leipzig, Germany; Prague, the Czech Republic; and Vienna, Austria. It's another dream come true. Stop wasting time and start working on your dreams.

7. GUARD YOUR MIND.

> *I will not let someone walk through*
> *my mind with their dirty feet.*
> —Mahatma Gandhi

When you guard against negativity and embrace positive thoughts, your mind will lead you to optimal outcomes. There are things that you can change and things that you cannot. Protect your mind from the negativity "viruses" that keep you from realizing your full potential.

In her book, *13 Things Mentally Strong People Don't Do*, author Amy Morin outlines thirteen thoughts and actions to avoid to kick bad mental habits and toughen yourself up. These include:

1. *Don't feel the world owes you anything*
2. *Don't give up after the first failure*
3. *Don't dwell on the past*
4. *Don't worry about pleasing everyone*
5. *Don't focus on things you can't control*
6. *Don't waste time feeling sorry for yourself*
7. *Don't expect immediate results*
8. *Don't fear taking a calculated risk*
9. *Don't shy away from change*
10. *Don't make the same mistakes over and over*
11. *Don't fear alone time*
12. *Don't resent other peoples' success*
13. *Don't give away your power*

If you find yourself falling into one of these mental traps, move on and get out of it!

8. REMOVE THE DEAD WEIGHT.

Have you ever worked with someone who, when they were absent, things ran more smoothly? There is no clearer sign of dead weight. This person is a burden. You most likely would be better off without them. The pandemic lockdowns forced us to remove unnecessary activities from our lives. It helped us to realize what we missed, what we didn't miss, what is of value, and what is dead weight.

If you just keep doing the same thing over and over again, you will not grow. Being satisfied with your current condition, with little desire for change, is *complacency*. When it comes to office management, this attitude leads to sloppiness and practice decline.

It is helpful to remove the things that take more than they give. This applies to activities and people. I've known a few. These people waste time, money, and opportunity. Add to the list bullies, negative coworkers, and naysayers. Eliminate them and make room for people who truly care about you and celebrate your successes.

So, take an inventory of what extra weight you've been carrying around like a ball and chain. Ask yourself, "Why am I doing this?" It could be parental influence. It could be religion. It could be force of habit. It could be lack of courage to face reality. Set yourself free!

9. THREE REMEDIES TO INCREASE PRODUCTIVITY

My husband and son tell me that I talk too much. They are both the quiet types. I am talkative. I am self-aware of my situation and my surroundings. I have taken up new, quiet hobbies such as gardening and jigsaw puzzles, which fit our home environment. Are you aware of how you mesh with the personality types in your office or shared environment?

When at my front desk, Lyndsay was ambitious and effective beyond compare. The negative side of this was that she can be, dare I say, bossy? She likes to work alone. She enjoys working uninterrupted, which has been found to be very efficient. She now works off-site from home and this change of venue has been a further win-win.

Jessica and Leona are relaxed and rational. They are peacemakers. We often praise Leona on her emotional intelligence. The negative side of this trait is that they do not speak up as often as other members of the team.

Jolene is a thoughtful planner. She is excellent as an inventory coordinator. She is a perfectionist with her orders. The negative side of this persona is that she can be a little critical of others.

Fortunately, all these personalities blend perfectly together. In areas where someone is weak, another is strong. The team is balanced.

Knowing the strengths and weaknesses of yourself and your staff will help you to use your skills most productively. Accurately assessing traits also helps you to understand each other.

Harmonization of group dynamics is also essential for nonprofits and boards of directors of dental organizations. Some members just don't care. The appointment is just a status symbol for them. They really don't want to attend the meetings or, in fact, do anything. Because it is a volunteer group, there is nothing that can be done about it. You have to accept it. Don't take it personally. Focus on what you can do.

Some believe that too many meetings destroy morale. In a TED Talk, Jason Fried suggests three remedies to increase productivity:

1. *No talking. Declare a quiet time.*
2. *Switch from active communication to passive, such as email or texting.*
3. *Cancel unnecessary meetings.*

Today's workplace is increasingly diverse, which is a good thing. The flip side is that we must work hard to be unified. As a team, we celebrate our uniqueness but focus on our similarities. We're all in it together. This is the idea of belonging. Everyone is included. Togetherness is our ultimate goal.

10. *IMPROVE YOUR SITUATION.*

Dental interns are easy to train, as their minds are like a sponge, soaking up everything that you teach them. In an orthodontic office, new staff usually start at the position of a sterilization coordinator. Next, they set up clinical deliveries. Then, they assist in the bonding and banding of braces. Next, if they have the inclination, they start learning the front desk and scheduling appointments. They answer the phones. They may learn to write patient contracts, obtain an X-ray license, and become a registered dental assistant.

The last step in learning for a dental assistant is to bill insurance. Doing this is perhaps the most painstaking, yet the most important job in the office. It is a full-time position. Having mastered all of these skills, the employee is probably the financial coordinator of the office and perhaps the highest-paid assistant. All that is left now is management. If you have a big team, ten to thirty or more, you may have a dental office manager.

Dentists always strive to learn more. We complete fellowships, become board certified, join study clubs, continue our pursuit of dental practice management, and even write articles or books. All that we absorb enables us to make better decisions. Sharing what we have learned makes patients and the entire profession better.

11. PURSUE MENTORSHIP.

As iron sharpens iron, so one person sharpens another.
                                                    –Proverbs 27:17

You might be wondering how it came to be that I published my first book. My father was a college professor who had written a textbook, *Metal Cutting Theory*. He was a mechanical engineer who specialized in industrial engineering. He believed that, by age fifty, everyone had a book in them from which another individual could benefit. I used to call my father in Massachusetts on my drive to work in California. He loved to hear about special marketing activities we were doing for our patients. He also felt that since I had grown my orthodontic practice from scratch to $1.8 million in revenue in seven years, my promotional ideas could help other orthodontists build their offices. He felt that my experiences could give others confidence and comfort. With his inspiration, I wrote the marketing book *It All Starts with Marketing: 201 Marketing Tips for Growing a Dental Practice.*

One evening while browsing in my hometown Barnes and Noble bookstore, I came across a social media book written by Patrick Schwerdtfeger and I noticed that his biography noted that he also lived in Walnut Creek. I thought, "Hey, this guy could teach me how to get a book published!" I sent him an email and invited him to lunch.

Notice that my tip reads, "pursue" mentorship. A mentor is not going to walk up to you and say, "Hey, can I be your mentor?" You must actively seek out mentorship if you want advice from a high-caliber individual. Take the first step. Pick up the phone or send an email. It never hurts to ask.

A mentor can teach you what you don't know. Patrick introduced me to my publisher, Stephanie Chandler at Authority Publishing, and the rest is history. Learning lessons the hard way can be avoided by adding a mentor to your life. Overconfidence, combined with inexperience, can lead to costly mistakes. Find someone whom you would like as a mentor. Then be bold and reach out.

CASE STUDY 12: THE GO-GETTER

Iris had just graduated from her orthodontic residency program. She had decided to stick around the university, accept a small orthodontic faculty position, and pursue a PhD in oral biology. To maintain her orthodontic skills, she wanted an associateship in a private office.

Iris knew that life is short. Looking for an associateship, she decided to start at the top and work her way down. She had read one orthodontist's textbook and also admired him as editor of a journal. She thought that working with him would be a dream come true. So, Iris picked up the phone and gave the orthodontist a call.

"Hello, may I please speak with the doctor?"

"Yes, this is the doctor."

Wow! Iris was amazed that she actually got through to the doctor. So, she double-checked. "Is this really the doctor, the orthodontist?"

"No, it's the president of the United States, what do you want?!"

"I want a job. I have just graduated from my residency and I am looking for an associateship. I would love to work with you."

"Would you now? OK, come on down to my office and we'll talk! Can you be here Tuesday during lunchtime?"

Iris got the job.

Solution:

Ask and you shall receive. You have nothing to lose.

This is the story of me and my mentor, Dr. T. M. Graber. I worked with Dr. Graber for one year before moving to California. The impact that this experience had on my life was unmeasurable. He encouraged me to achieve my American Board of Orthodontics diplomate status, and he challenged me to join the Edward H. Angle Society of Orthodontists. He believed in me, and I couldn't let him down. To this day, his memory still gives me inspiration.

I remember one of Dr. Graber's favorite sayings: "Don't let the turkeys get you down." Dr. Graber knew that there were naysayers, pessimists, and downright mean-spirited people out there. I'm sure that he experienced a few during his professional journey. He never let anyone hold him back. Dr. Graber always had a smile on his face. It was an honor to have known him.

Case Study 13: Create Your Own Future

The doctor received notice that he would no longer be the editor of the journal. He was upset. He exclaimed, "What do they think, that I am going to die?" He was eighty-four years old.

Nonetheless, the doctor was not going to let this news get him down. He declared, "I'll start a new journal! It will be an international journal. And, it will have color photos!"

Solution:

Lift yourself up and move on to new opportunities. These open doors may prove to be better than those that shut behind you. As you may have guessed, this individual was also Dr. Graber.

12. Make decisions that produce.

> You cannot make progress without making decisions.
> –Jim Rohn

None of us want to waste time and money. This is why team meetings are important. We need to discuss and analyze business tactics: what is producing results, what is not, what we should stick with, and what we should drop.

Do your homework. Strategize. Plan your day. Design your life.

13. Do whatever it takes.

Grit—the unrelenting desire to succeed.
–Nick Hays

In 1967, a twelve-year-old boy called the president of Hewlett-Packard, Bill Hewlett, at his Palo Alto home and asked if he had any spare parts for a frequency counter that he wanted to build. Hewlett gave him the spare parts. He also gave him a summer job at Hewlett-Packard putting nuts and bolts into frequency counters. High school student Steve Jobs would later recount, "I was in heaven. Most people don't get these experiences because they never ask."

Be willing to fight for what you want. No one is going to hand it over to you. Grit and persistence lead to triumph. Believe in yourself and stay focused. Never stop until you cross the finish line. Identify the things that are actively opposing you, the things that are intentionally undermining you, and eliminate them. A great attitude and not searching for others' approval are two strong ingredients for success.

Chapter 12

ENERGY

Relationships are based on four principles:
respect, understanding, acceptance, and appreciation.
                                    –Mahatma Gandhi

There is no more beautiful sound in my office than when I hear a patient whose treatment I just completed talking and laughing with my financial coordinator at the front desk. This is the sound of patient joy. It is the sound of a team win. When you think of team energy, you think of a certain "vibe." What is the spirit that your team exudes?

Being together with a group of high-spirited individuals can be gratifying, no matter what the job. In fact, it can be one of the most rewarding experiences of your life. The energy of a team catalyzes individual effort. With an energized team, untapped talent is unleashed.

GRATITUDE

Gratitude can transform common days into thanksgivings,
turn routine jobs into joy,
and change ordinary opportunities into blessings.
–William Arthur Ward

When it comes to types of positive energy, let's start with gratitude. It is impossible to be simultaneously negative and be grateful. I once took my team on a quarterly outing to have lunch at our local golf course. As we ate out on the patio, we reflected on our thankfulness. I gifted each staff member a gratitude journal to help them remember this day, this team, this time, and those things for which they gave thanks.

During the pandemic, we felt extreme gratitude for our jobs. I felt grateful to be a health care provider and to continue to care for patients who needed us. We are essential workers. Gratitude gave us the fortitude to go on.

Our patients are loyal to us. They wait to see us. We are also loyal to our patients and to each other. Not only does gratitude connect our team, but it also fuels our growth. Instead of focusing on setbacks, focusing on gratitude for what you can control and improve will provide renewed energy for your practice.

THREE PHRASES OF AFFIRMATION

Nothing else can quite substitute for
a few well-chosen, well-timed, sincere words of praise.
They're absolutely free and worth a fortune.
–Sam Walton

In their book, *The 5 Languages of Appreciation in the Workplace: Empowering Organizations by Encouraging People,* authors and relationship psychologists Gary Chapman and Paul White write that words of affirmation are the most frequent form of gratitude at work at a rate of forty-five percent. If you want to give a shout out to someone on your team, here are three phrases with which to start:

"*I appreciate you.*"

Words of affirmation make everyone's day. They are both a joy for the receiver and the giver. As a leader, it is important to let your team members individually know that they are doing a great job and that their efforts are appreciated.

"*I admire you.*"

Everyone has qualities that others can admire. It could be their personality, optimism, or humor. It may be how they work. They may be focused, organized, or neat. They may be an inspiration, or a cheerleader for others. They may be motivational. Whatever makes each team member special, let them know.

"*You belong here.*"

In his book, *The Culture Code: The Secrets of Highly Successful Groups*, author Daniel Coyle states that belonging cues answer the ancient question, "Am I safe here?" A true sense of belonging gives your body and mind the answer, "Don't worry, everything will be alright."

Belonging cues include proximity, eye contact, positive energy, mimicry, turn-taking, attention, body language, vocal pitch, and whether everyone talks to everyone else in the group. A feeling of belonging tells our brains to stop worrying about dangers and instead shift to the mode of psychological safety, where work can truly begin. The opposite of "belonging" is actually "othering," a belief that a person does not fit in, i. e., is not part of the team. As captain, you must strive to eliminate alienation in favor of alignment for team dynamics to shine.

WRITTEN WORDS

According to *The Culture Code*, a handwritten note of encouragement is a powerful belonging cue. It can inspire, give energy, or even make someone smarter.

I was intrigued by this concept. So, I tried it on my own team. I wrote everyone a personalized, appreciative, and motivational note. It read:

"You are doing a great job. I know that we will be able to reach or surpass our goals this month with your contribution. Keep up the great work."

To my pleasant surprise, our production numbers went up 212 percent from the year prior! This intervention was so effective that I am going to stop writing right now and send each of my team members a note!

Dr. Gregory Walton of Stanford University states that the little nudge of a note signals connection that totally transforms the way that people relate, how they feel, and how they behave. Do it! Write each and every one of your employees a personal note of affirmative appreciation right now. See what happens. You will not be disappointed!

QUALITY TIME

Just because a team member values Quality Time
doesn't mean they want time with the boss.
Many people enjoy time with their colleagues.
–Gary Chapman and Paul White

Every three months, I take my team out for lunch. It is a time for me to say "thank you" for their work and being part of our office. Here we unwind, trade stories, get to know each other's interests, likes, dislikes, and share our personal lives. This helps us to understand each other better. It also builds trust and vulnerability.

Thinking back on my years playing tennis on the San Francisco City College tennis team, what I cherished most was our time together traveling to matches in the team van. The conversations were fun. We got to know each other and my teammates simply liked me for being me. We would talk and laugh until our stomachs hurt. This was a special time, a relaxed environment, a place of total acceptance, which is what we aspire to achieve with our teams. This environment of peace takes time and social relaxation to develop. The leader doesn't necessarily need to be there. In fact, when I think back to those days in the tennis team van, the coach rarely participated in the conversation. She sat there quietly driving. Next time that you take your team out to lunch, or on a CE trip, excuse yourself and give the team time on their own to bond.

Voluntary, unpaid time to socialize shows your staff that you truly enjoy their company. You're teammates in the office and outside of it. Often for our team Christmas parties, we rent a limousine and drive to a distant location. These road trips have been some of the most memorable occasions for my team. I always tell them, "These are the times that you will remember because these are the times that we all celebrated together."

Two Pillars of Happiness

Every day, the happy person does at least one difficult thing.
        –Mihaly Csikszentmihalyi

Running a dental practice can be difficult at times. It can also be one of the most fun jobs in the world. I love going to my office and I'm excited when the work week begins. I literally can't wait to see my patients. I am thrilled when a patient starts treatment. Holding my weekly team meeting and sharing something new with my team, such as a new book, a new project, or a new idea, is very enjoyable for me. I love giving our patients a beautiful smile. I'm grateful for the impact that a smile has on their lives. I feel that this is what God put me on this earth to do (besides writing this book): give patients a smile. Add to this the freedom and financial equity of dental practice ownership, and I think, "What job on earth could be better?"

Happy team members are more productive and possess better attitudes, greater attendance, higher morale, and lower turnover. Understanding what makes people happy is therefore good for business. Strong interpersonal relationships are correlated with happiness. Gainful employment makes people happy, especially when one loves their job.

In his book, *Good Business: Leadership, Flow, and the Making of Meaning*, research psychologist Mihaly Csikszentmihalyi discusses that fulfilling one's highest potential, which usually generates happiness, depends on the presence of two processes.

The first process is the self-realization of **differentiation**, the understanding that *we are each unique* and we individually are responsible for our own survival and well-being. Those who are willing to accept and develop their own uniqueness will enjoy its expression.

The second process is one of **integration**, development of our social network, and the realization that *we choose our relationships*, we have cultural symbols in which we delight, and we co-create our work environment.

A person who is both *differentiated* and *integrated* becomes a *complex individual.* Those who fulfill both of these requirements have the best chance of leading a happy life of fulfillment.

It may be impossible to survive in dentistry or as the leader of a dental team without enjoying what one does. Without the joy, the job would be too stressful, the hours too long, and the work, drudgery. We strive to have everyone on our team, including ourselves, find deep satisfaction and meaning in their work. Happiness is that exhilarating feeling that results from being fully alive.

ALL IN

> *Wherever you go, go with all your heart.*
> –Confucius

When you are in the moment, focused on the task at hand, the problems of everyday life have no chance of registering in your mind. Control is no problem. You're in the zone. You're in a state of flow.

Mihaly Csikszentmihalyi has shown that the happy state of flow is achieved when one is most focused. There is a loss of ego, forgetting of problems and surroundings, and a loss of one's very self. You're happy in the moment. Challenge and skill are high. Goals are clear. Feedback is immediate. When this happens, your patient does well, you do well, and your office does well. Four hours seem like ten minutes.

The opposite of flow is apathy, which leads to sadness, anxiety, and depression. Near to this are boredom and worry. All of these emotional states produce stress. Apathetically working without focus or challenge, just going through the motions of job tasks, will result in the dead end of burnout.

In order for your team members to feel happiness in their jobs, they must feel in control. They must be "all in." So, ask them, **"Are we all in?"** They must be in charge of the goals, of the work that they do, and of every step of their performance. When metrics are clear and the team member is focused on achieving that goal—their goal—there is no management or, heaven forbid, "micromanagement" necessary or desired.

We all have the capacity to produce these best environmental factors for achieving happiness at work. To enable flow, set clear benchmarks, provide an individual sense of control and flexible use of time, balance skill sets with challenges, and give feedback and praise. Maintaining a reservoir of human happiness will nourish your office's financial bottom line.

THREE QUESTIONS TO REVIEW EXPECTATIONS

CEO of the Los Angeles-based executive coaching firm, Ferrazzi Greenlight, and author of the book, *Leading Without Authority: How the New Power of Co-Elevation Can Break Down Silos, Transform Teams, and Reinvent Collaboration*, Keith Ferrazzi pushes for peer-to-peer accountability and mutual support to reach desired end results. By holding members responsible, the entire organization is taken a notch higher. Ferrazzi states that, as leader, your job is to make sure that your team understands that each person on the team is accountable for their own tasks.

To begin this process, write down your expected outcomes. This makes them real. Distribute the goals. Review your results weekly and track progress until you realize your aims. Give credit for the results to your team, who will learn a tremendous amount by participating in this process. Mistakes will be mended. Difficulties will be solved. Learning and growth will take place. Teamwork will be improved. Here are three questions that you can ask to review expectations:

> *Did we get done what we needed to get done?*
>
> *Is anyone struggling?*
>
> *What are we going to do today, and next week, to help us reach our goals?*

We all need relationship action plans when working on a team. Ask yourself:

> *Do you really know everyone on your team?*
>
> *Do you work well with everyone on your team?*
>
> *Whose support do you need to be successful?*

FIVE STATES OF CO-ELEVATION

Get working on building those relationships. Keith Ferrazzi devised a system while working as a young executive at Deloitte, which he calls "the co-elevation continuum." Score your inter-relationships at work:

- **+2 Co-elevation**
- **+1 Collaboration**
- **0 Co-exist**
- **-1 Resist**
- **-2 Resentment**

Most relationships reside at the "Co-exist" level: people working together to get their job done but respectfully staying out of each other's way. At times, however, we must work with others on the team to accomplish what we need to get done. We need help or resources not under our control. Partnering with others, we move to a +1 "Collaborative" or +2 "Co-elevation" state. It's a win-win situation, an ideal, mutually beneficial arrangement. It's not your way or my way; it's a better way, a higher way, of interacting.

What if things don't go well? Collaboration becomes challenging. We feel tension or stress when dealing with a colleague. We passively or subconsciously avoid cooperation—even when it would boost our own success. We are now at -1 "Resist" status. If things really head south, we may become frustrated with our co-worker. We are left with only surface attempts to save in public. Jack Welch called this "superficial congeniality." The relationship is now in a -2 "Resentment" level, a passive-aggressive, lose-lose situation.

What can be done to fix these nonideal interactions? Try this:

"I'm embarrassed to say that I haven't really engaged you as much as I should have. I would love to work together on this project."

By aiming for co-elevation into your culture, you will be able to break down silos and cliques by initiating collaborative teamwork that will propel your organization forward.

Don't waste time trying to co-elevate resisters. Start with the positive people first. The resisters will come around once they start seeing the results. Then they will want to join in on the fun.

BELIEF

> *Leadership is a transfer of belief.*
> –Jon Gordon

Who would have thought that we would have iPhones, iCloud, or an Apple watch? Steve Jobs believed that these dreams were possible. With Jobs' distorted optimism, his teams accomplished what was originally thought to be impossible. A leader re-defines reality, distorting it in a positive way. What could your group achieve if they shared your outlook and belief in what is achievable?

Try this exercise. Ask each team member, *"What could we do to make these goals possible?"* Leverage their ideas and ingenuity to make your goals your reality.

ENCOURAGEMENT

"I believe in you."
Those four words can mean the difference between
a fear of failure and the courage to try.

–Coach K

Words matter. They can make the difference between motivation and discouragement, courage and fear, optimism and pessimism.

When highly-motivated, energized, and united, nothing can compare to the unbridled energy of a cohesive team working together. So, choose your words wisely. Keep the positive energy flowing.

Actions matter. Whether a high five, low five, or elbow bump, our body language can express "Way to go!" or "Well done!" We can place a hand on a teammate's shoulder as a sign of care, concern, and empathy. Human beings need reinforcement and encouragement.

Positive energy is never forgotten. I still have my two San Francisco City College tennis team photos in my personal orthodontic office as a remembrance of happy team times. Once a year, I declare a "Team Day" and take the annual office photo. Make sure that everyone gets a copy. This is a keepsake of teamwork, encouragement, and remembrance of happy times together for each member of your team.

In their book, *The 5 Languages of Appreciation in the Workplace,* Gary Chapman and Paul White express that only six percent of employees choose tangible gifts as their primary language of appreciation, while sixty-eight percent report that it is their least-valued form of acknowledgement. So, when you truly want to make someone's day, simply saying, "Great Job!" or, "I appreciate your hard work," or, "I like the way you do that," might just be the best reward and encouragement that you could ever give.

Chapter 13

TOGETHER

Effective teamwork begins and ends with communication.

–Coach K

The life cycle of a team has been described as, "forming, storming, norming, performing." In his book, *Leading Teams: Setting the Stage for Great Performances*, social and organizational psychologist J. Richard Hackman of Harvard University states that it is nearly impossible to get a new team to have a worthwhile discussion of performance strategy at the start of working together. So jump right in and get started. Get some experience. Then, refine strategy from there.

We know that teamwork is the foundation of a successful dental office and being a team player is one of the requirements of employment. Building a winning organization starts with careful selection of your players, front and back office. Next comes communication about what it is going to take to win.

FIVE ON-BOARDING ACTIONS

Day one of employment is initiation. Make this day memorable by giving your new team member signs of belonging. Here are five items to build loyalty and belonging.

1. REVIEW OF THE TEAM HANDBOOK

Pay your new hire to sit for one hour and read your Team Handbook. Have them sign a declaration of receipt and understanding. The team will refer to this Handbook many times through the years when employment protocol and behavior questions arise.

2. ISSUING OF THE TEAM UNIFORM

A uniform is a form of unity training that conveys an immediate sign of acceptance and belonging. The uniform states, "You're part of our team," and, "We expect you to stay." I can't tell you how excited my staff is to order a new uniform style. We have a different team uniform for each day of the week. Team uniforms say, "We all count," and, "We're all in this together."

3. TAKING A NEW TEAM PHOTO

Place your new team member's professional photo on the wall with an engraved name plate. Everyone who enters the office now sees their picture and knows their name. This is a sign of accepting team responsibility, but also a source of individual pride.

Have a team group photo done at least once per year. You want your team to look sharp! It's also a nice memento for a retiring team member, especially when everyone signs the photo before framing. The team photo can also be used on your website and in your marketing.

4. ISSUING THE TEAM MEMBER NAME TAG

Have a new team member's name tag ready on day one. Wearing a name tag is a Delta Dental requirement. Wear your name tag on the right side of your shirt or lab jacket so that when someone shakes your hand, they are looking diagonally at your name. It also helps to create a welcoming and professional office environment.

5. RECEIVING THE TEAM MEMBER BUSINESS CARD

The first day on a job is meant to be memorable. The new team member will give their personalized business card to all their family and friends that night when they return home. A personal business card tells the new team member, "We're excited to have you on our team."

This "Welcome Aboard" program can give even the twenty-year veteran a bit of gung-ho enthusiasm of a newcomer.

TEN QUALITIES OF AN IDEAL TEAM PLAYER

When people do what they love, they get up in the morning and say, "I can't wait to get to work!" Assuming that people have the requisite technical skills, what other qualities do you look for in an ideal team player? New staff must enhance the team by contributing their own "right stuff."

1. RELIABLE

> *Eighty percent of success is showing up.*
> –Woody Allen

If your team member doesn't show up, nothing else matters. Face it, you can't work alone. **You must have reliable team members.** This holds true for being on time, having consistent attendance, and giving advanced notice about appointments, vacations, and other absences.

One effective way to reinforce attendance is the "Vacation Request Form." If a team member plans a day or week off, the notice is given at a minimum of six weeks in advance. On the form, the team member gets a signature from whomever will provide cross coverage during the absence. The form is then given to the doctor to sign for final approval. Everyone knows about the absence well ahead of time. The form is put in the team member's HR folder. Clear communication about the value of reliability is the best policy.

CASE STUDY 14: THE RELIABLE

A resume arrived in response to an employment ad on Indeed. At the top was written, "I am reliable." Polly had no dental office experience but those key words alone warranted an interview. She was an older woman who had raised two grown sons and was recently divorced. She had held two jobs during her lifetime, one for nineteen years and one for seventeen years. Her place of recent employment had closed. Polly stated that it had been difficult for her to find a job because of her age. Her primary purpose for finding employment was to get out of the house.

Solution:

Polly was hired part-time. She later became a full-time front desk receptionist. She learned to schedule appointments. During her tenure, she never missed a day of work. Reliability outdoes skill and experience every time. Reliability is the bedrock standard of employment.

2. HONEST

A team player who is an honest communicator will keep everyone in the loop. They are trusted. There are no secrets and no unwanted surprises.

Much of the communication amongst staff takes place informally. Beyond the formal weekly team meeting, good team players feel comfortable talking with each other throughout the day, passing on important information about what is going on in the office. Good team players are honest and vulnerable in sharing their views. They share updates, knowledge, experiences, and even cookies!

3. ENGAGED

There is no "dead weight" on an outstanding team. Every member is valuable by virtue of contributing their own unique talents. Engaged employees come to meetings prepared, having done their preparation. They do not sit passively on the sidelines. They listen actively and speak up during discussions. They are fully engaged.

Active team players cooperate and help. They are agreeable to the activities of the office and the requests of the leader/doctor. They don't say "I'm busy" when assistance is requested. On the contrary, they take initiative to help without being told.

These excellent team players have a "can-do" attitude. They act in the moment. They ask themselves daily, "What can I do to make the team a success?"

4. SUPPORTIVE

Supportive team members ask others for their opinion. They are aware of, and sensitive to, others' needs. Great team players don't place conditions on when or where they will help or not help. They are not territorial. They don't say, "That's not my job," or "That's not your job." They help out wherever and whenever they can.

5. CONSTRUCTIVE

Don't shoot the messenger. Be grateful for the truth, or dare I say, "constructive criticism." Having candor is the basis of effective communication. Constructive team members are not afraid to make a point for the good of the office. They express themselves in a positive, confident, and respectful manner.

6. SOLUTION ORIENTED

> *Be a problem solver, not a problem bringer.*
> —Jay Abraham

Problem solvers don't point fingers or place blame on others when things don't go right. Solvers resolve the bad, and celebrate the good. They act on what they can do to create a solution. With problem solvers, strategies and action plans are generated.

A great team player is a problem solver, not a problem creator. A great team player is not a problem avoider. They know that problems are a part of life. This includes having the backs of their team members and leader in times of difficulty.

The language of a problem solver may be the following: "We've done a great job defining the problem. How can we work together to solve it?"

7. RESPECTFUL

Great team players treat their co-workers with respect, including thoughtful listening. They know that everyone's opinion counts. They never exclude other team members or, heaven forbid, give "the silent treatment." Everyone is included and belongs. Everyone counts. Great team players are fun to be around and never have fun at someone else's expense. Simply put, they are professional.

8. FLEXIBLE

> *It is not the strongest of the species that survives,*
> *nor the most intelligent.*
> *It is the one that is most adaptable to change.*
> —Charles Darwin

Great team players are flexible to the demands of the team. They know how to deal with changing conditions. Such individuals know that life is unpredictable and not perfect. They are up for all challenges. They adapt.

Flexible team players don't hold rigid viewpoints. They consider the perspectives of others and are open to what others have to offer. They are flexible in pitching in with the team to achieve success.

9. A LISTENER

> *Listening is communicating.*
> —Jon Gordon

The most valuable team player may well be a communicator who is perhaps not the most eloquent speaker but who has the ability to listen, process information, and provide good feedback. The best listeners are capable of truly understanding what a person is trying to convey. They seek first to understand, then to be understood. They don't interrupt. Better yet, they make the speaker feel and know that they are heard.

This is perhaps the hardest team quality of all: to listen. A great team player listens, absorbs, understands, and considers everyone's ideas and points of view. This is the essence of "active" listening.

A listening team player is also open to constructive advice on how to improve. They are trainable. They do not get defensive when shown how to become better. This outstanding team player quality includes the discipline to listen first and to speak second. With a bona fide listener, a meaningful and effective discussion leads to actions that produce results.

10. COMMITTED

Commitment requires sacrifice.
                                        –Jon Gordon

Strong team players don't want to let down their colleagues. They care not only about their own work, but also about each other. Great team players don't necessarily need to be "rah-rah cheerleader" types. They may be soft-spoken, but their attendance and consistency are conscientious acts that speak louder than words. They need not be pushed to be a team player. They are naturally committed and "all in" at all times.

Team players look beyond themselves. They want the organization to succeed. They are persistent. Being able to win as a team is one of their greatest motivators.

CASE STUDY 15: THE NO-SHOW

Emily didn't show up for work regularly. She did not attend the quarterly team social outing either. It was at a favorite local restaurant, chosen by the team, to celebrate something special, to kick back, relax, and enjoy each other's company. It was the gift of togetherness. Emily thought that it was a waste of her time.

Solution:

When someone's actions say, "I don't care about you or being a member of this team," it's a bad sign. This person already has one foot out the door to their next job. Explain to this employee that their relationships in the office are important. Ask them why they do not attend events. Ask them how they would like it if others did not attend their special event someday.

When someone does not come to work, letting down the patients and the team, it is an ominous signal. They are isolating themselves from the team. They may be disgruntled. They are indicating their preference not to waste their time making an emotional commitment with this group of people. You must treat absenteeism very seriously and plan accordingly.

This lack of commitment portends future quitting by the employee or dismissal by the doctor and team.

FIVE TEAMWORK ACTIONS

> *A group becomes a team when each member*
> *is sure enough of himself and his contribution*
> *to praise the skill of others.*
>
> –Norman Shidle

1. MAKE HIGH-QUALITY DECISIONS TOGETHER.

It should be no surprise to anyone in the office when a new member is chosen for the team. Everyone on the existing team had the opportunity to weigh in on selecting the new candidate. After the first working interview, the staff had the opportunity to take the prospect out to lunch without the doctor. Then the group met with the doctor to share their thoughts about the candidate. If there was unanimous agreement that this individual would be an excellent addition to the team, then a second working interview was done to confirm that everyone's assessment, including the doctor's, was accurate.

The high-quality decision of accepting a new team member is not rushed. It takes a minimum of two weeks, and in general, it takes one month. If no reasonable candidate is found, the search continues until a fit is found. Finally, when the search is done, everyone pitches in to help the new team member to be a success. The entire team made this pivotal high-quality decision together.

2. ENCOURAGE THE TEAM AND TAKE REASONABLE RISKS.

I once heard a dental podcast with Katherine Eitel Belt, owner of LionSpeak, a company that helps professionals to communicate with more authenticity and effectiveness. Katherine advocated, "The next time you think 'How can I tell her?' think 'How can I not tell her?'" I've been using this form of open communication with the team and encouraging them to use it with me and each other ever since.

Courage, communication, and candor are the prerequisites needed to take reasonable risks. Open communication about what can be improved and be achieved allows the team to be the very best that it can be.

3. CONDUCT 360-DEGREE REVIEWS.

There is no better place to brainstorm suggestions for improvements to the office than at the annual 360 reviews. Here are questions that can be asked:

1. *What does this team member do best?*
2. *What could this person improve?*
3. *What can this employee work on in the coming year?*

Team members can anonymously complete this questionnaire for themselves, for each teammate, and for the doctor. The results can be collated by the doctor and privately reviewed with each individual by the doctor, by an HR professional, or by the HR coordinator of the office. This is an excellent method for each individual to say what needs to be said, without fear of retaliation, with an aim to maximize improvement of the individual and the office.

4. EXPECT AND ENCOURAGE DIFFERENT VIEWPOINTS.

The more viewpoints, the fresher the ideas, the stronger the team will be. We all have different backgrounds, experiences, and opinions. Everyone needs to be included since everyone's input matters. For a strong team, encourage the open exchange of ideas. This builds vulnerability and trust among team members and gives staff the courage to try. Make it clear that your office is an open and safe environment where there is nothing to fear in being your true self.

5. KEEP COMMUNICATING.

It's the start of a new year. The team meets for the annual advance, a day of togetherness, brainstorming, reflection, and planning. Leaders know that it is their job to motivate the team, to maintain a strong work ethic, and to build enthusiasm for the months ahead. Below is an example of what could be said as an introduction, to foster a culture of communication:

"Our business either grows or shrinks by what we do each day. Our future success depends on each and every one of us working together.

"We share the vision: smiles change lives. Otherwise, why be here? We live this vision, doing the work necessary to give our patients the smile of their dreams, and the great experience which they deserve.

"Everyone here is on the same team. Each person is empowered to make a difference for our patients and for each other. When the practice succeeds, everyone succeeds. Each person on our team agrees that the challenges that we face together are part of a shared responsibility and that all problems can be solved.

"We plan not to just succeed, but to succeed greatly. To accomplish this goal, we need to work together.

"There are many referring dentists who will continue to send us patients because of our work this past year. We need to continue to have strong relationships with every dental practice in our community.

"There are new families moving to our community every day. We need to reach out to them.

"We have many happy patients who want to send their family and friends to us. We need to give them the tools that they need to make referring to our office easy.

"We need to keep active with the community in outreach and public relations programs.

"We need to keep doing our jobs with excellence, kindness, friendliness, and a positive and professional attitude for our team and our office to be a success.

"Our teamwork will provide the best patient experience possible. We're open and honest about our goals and we all know our individual and office target numbers. There's no reason why we can't all achieve our goals and celebrate together again next year.

"To function as a winning team, we need to work smart and not take minor misunderstandings personally. This past year, we achieved success, but nothing is as important as now and the future. We want to make the most of every day.

"Our office could not deliver ideal care if not for each and every one of us. Today, at our annual advance, we will discuss our past year's numbers and review our forward-facing goals. Numbers are the *language of our business and will help us to build our future working together.*

"Let us not forget the integrity, professionalism, hard work, respect, service, dedication, teamwork, and leadership which helped us to be successful. These words describe each and every one of us. These qualities are what we are all about.

"What we do together makes a difference for our patients, for our community, for our referring doctors, and for our families, ourselves, and our world. Thank you for being part of our special team.

"As your leader, I am dedicated to making the next ten years the best for each and every one of us. I hope you will join me in making this year our best year ever. It's going to be exciting and fun. Then next year at this time, we can once again celebrate what we have achieved working together."

A TEAM THAT HAS GELLED

> *To me, teamwork is the beauty of our sport,*
> *where you have five acting as one.*
> *You become selfless.*
> –Coach K

Here is a profound statement: the team is only as strong as the teamwork of the superstar player. The weakest player may not be the problem. If you've ever been on a team with a prima donna, you know what I'm talking about. *A team* by definition is *a group of people working together for a common goal.* We want superstar performers to be team players.

Occasionally, one team member may lag behind. There is no greater motivator than encouragement by peers for someone to raise their game. This might even be characterized as "peer pressure." Through experience, I have found that once an issue is brought out into the open, it usually resolves quickly or the responsible individual quits: it's a "shape up or ship out" moment.

It's really up to the team to make the necessary improvements to achieve high performance. Let the team fix their people problems first. **No** *one will know more about what the team needs to be successful than the team itself.* At first, individuals may be afraid to speak up. The 360-degree reviews help. As the team leader, when you bring problems into the light for resolution, more issues will be solved. And, you will have built your ideal team in the process.

PART THREE

COLLABORATION

Coming together is beginning;
keeping together is progress;
working together is success.
–Henry Ford

It is through working together, particularly in outings, and sharing personal stories that the team and leader gel as an organization. Slowly, the team and leader adapt to each other as they endeavor collaboratively toward their common goal. With the addition of each new team member, the office either improves, moving forward to accomplishment, or declines, slipping backward to loss. It is the quality of the team's collaboration that will determine which direction the team will follow.

It will be the job of the leader to set, maintain, and enforce the desired standards to enhance the group's working culture code. It should be everyone's common goal to work together to achieve the highest quality performance possible.

Chapter 14

MANAGEMENT

Instead of micromanaging your employees,
empower them by providing clear direction
and guidance on priorities.

–Eric Strafel

A s a dental practice owner, turning over aspects of practice manage-ment to your staff is a little like leaving your child with the babysitter. There is a job to be done. And, you're going to need to check in periodi-cally to evaluate how it's going and to make sure that everything is up to your standards.

A level of performance and trust with your team members has already been established. The team is aligned. They may even be self-directing and not need a great deal of oversight. Everyone is in the right place doing the right job. Now, you are fine-tuning, and checking on achievement, and motivating the team to keep up the great work.

The ability to lead people personally is limited to X number of peo-ple. The number X will vary depending upon the leader. For a dentist who does not want to lead, X is zero. This person cannot even lead him-self. There is laissez-faire leadership, which is no leadership at all. This dentist would be better off hiring an office manager.

For a capable dentist astute in business management, the ideal num-ber of team members without a manager may be as high as thirty. Above this number, smaller groups start to form naturally, such as a back-office group, and a front-office group. Here, a manager may be a helpful liaison between the groups and the leader. The manager can assist the doctor by maintaining organization, communicating with members, and helping with general systems, such as payroll and human resource management.

FOUR FUNCTIONS OF MANAGEMENT

Management is the act of aligning people's
actions, behaviors, and attitudes
with the needs of the organization.
–Patrick Lencioni

Management brings order. The systems of management are to help ordinary people behaving in normal ways to complete routine jobs successfully. That's it. Management in this way is boring. Management is a "peacetime" endeavor.

Management includes planning, budgeting, and setting goals and strategies. Management achieves its goals by organizing people. Management dictates who will do what by assigning jobs and delegating responsibilities. Management monitors implementation of the plan. The results of management are reflected in reports. The end result of management is controlled evaluation and problem-solving.

Throughout the management process, emphasis is focused on four functions:

1. *Execute the work.*
2. *Monitor progress.*
3. *Fine-tune effectiveness.*
4. *Set future directions.*

MANAGER-LED TEAMS

Management is about persuading people
to do things they do not want to do,
while leadership is about inspiring people to do things
they never thought they could.

−Steve Jobs

A leader shapes the purpose and defines the goals of the team, while always focusing on the "Why." If part of the team, a manager often tends to focus on the "What" or end result, losing the motivational "big picture." Manager-led teams can waste time and money. When managers specify and control aspects of a team's work, the team may become more dysfunctional for both the members and the organization. When a leader takes a direct approach, resources are not wasted on a middleman and efficiency can be improved.

DEFINING AUTHORITY

Once the decision is made about who is hired and what role they play, the next step toward an effective team is to define authority. Teams can be too timid, not making self-directed decisions. Or, teams can overstep the bounds of team rules, playing "above their pay grade." In defining boundaries, the leader codifies what decisions team members are able to make.

For example, spending money is not a team decision. You may have an inventory coordinator, but there are boundaries as to how big any given order can be placed. Setting such limits of authority will require leaders to exercise their own leadership skill and emotional maturity.

Micromanagement

A boss who micromanages
is like a coach who wants to get in the game.
Leaders guide and support and then sit back
to cheer from the sidelines.

–Simon Sinek

As the leader of your practice or president of your dental society, it is your responsibility to know enough about what is going on to understand the systems needed to achieve results. As the leader, you are there to provide support. **A total "hands-off" approach risks team failure.** As the leader, if the team starts to falter, it is your job to jump in and help. When intervention is needed, it is not "micromanagement" for the leader to step in and lend a hand. It will be your job as leader to coach your team to make sure that they have a good plan in place, rectify the situation, and to achieve results.

You need to know about any small issues before they become big issues that might be too late to do anything about.

Involvement of the leader should not be perceived as a sign of lack of trust. Providing guidance can be vital to success. Every high-achieving athlete has a coach. Your dental office team or dental society board likewise will need direction. One rule of leadership which avoids micromanagement is summarized as, "Hands off, nose in."

It is a sign of neglect for a CEO, dental office owner, or president of a dental society to stop being involved. This is abdication of responsibility. On a self-governing team, such as a dental society board, members decide upon strategic goals and tactics of implementation. Even a highly cohesive working group will still benefit by holding themselves accountable, including being open to feedback.

Dental assistants are within the boundaries of a self-managing team. In between patients, they do work out of the doctor's sight. As long as their decisions are consistent with the office's overall direction, dental assisting teams are free to structure their work as they see fit. They are self-managing unless they need direction or help.

THE PETER RECYCLE PRINCIPLE

During Dr. Howard Farran's podcast "Dentistry Uncensored," I discuss a topic described in my last book, *Take Action: Treatment Coordination for a Successful Dental Practice*. It's called the Peter Principle, which states that, "In a hierarchy, every employee tends to rise to his level of incompetence." Howard Farran mentioned a job that he had in dental school that involved unloading packages delivered to FedEx. He enjoyed the physical work, which after a long day in the classroom provided him with a much-needed workout.

Because he excelled in unloading packages, Howard was then promoted to loading packages for the FedEx trucks. Now he needed to sort packages by zip code. Not knowing the zip codes of the area, he did not like this job! He was ultimately let go. He asked his employer, "Could I go back down to the job that I loved?" The employer said, "No." The only way to move was up.

Let's introduce the Peter Recycle Principle. Yes, it is possible, and sometimes desirable to reassign an employee to their former position. Here is the wording to use when you would like to reverse a promotion:

"Your skills look like you might be better suited for your previous job. You're not cutting it in this new area. We can't keep doing what we are presently doing. Let's move you back to your previous occupation at your previous pay rate where your performance was outstanding. Does that sound agreeable to you?"

Some people will not want to move back down. Their ego will have been hurt, and they will quit. Others will gladly go back to their previous job. Many of these people will continue to excel at what they were already doing well. We try to promote within our own dental teams. Sometimes, there is a limit to someone's skills, or what they can be taught, or what they want to do. Some clinical assistants, for example, are not assertive enough to be at the front desk. We need to accept this fact. No one wants a team member to struggle to a point of unhappiness in a job for which they are not suited.

FOUR STAGES OF TEAM DEVELOPMENT

In his book, *Leading Teams: Setting the Stage for Great Performances,* author J. Richard Hackman, professor of Social and Organization Psychology at Harvard University, states that team development has four stages as described by Tuckman: forming, storming, norming, and performing.

In the life cycle of your team or dental organization, you will experience this progression. This is also true for an existing team that may start new coaching or add a new team member. With each transition, the dynamics of the team changes and you will begin again. You may find the first two stages, forming and storming, difficult and stressful. But, once you get through to stages three and four, norming and performing, you will feel the exhilaration of teamwork success.

1. FORMING

The coming together of a new group is challenging. You ultimately need to establish roles, rules, and behavioral norms. Clarity is essential. Leadership is needed. There will be personalities, pushback, and egos. **The leader must remain strong.** Laissez-faire leadership will engender a culture of "anything goes," and there will be chaos, lack of organization and alignment, and little performance.

You want members of the team to stay for a considerable amount of time. This is especially true for volunteer organizations. Usually, there is a set pattern of ascension: task assignment, membership chair, secretary, treasurer, vice president, and president. The time period at each step may be set for one or two years. On such a pathway, members are encouraged to remain a part of the group because they are rising in the ranks of leadership. **Commitment is stronger when ascension within the organization is transparent and fair.**

It is the same in your dental office. When you have an existing team, your dedicated people may want to apply for a new, higher-level position. It is best to have a fair, just, and ethical employment process that provides equal opportunity to grow professionally.

Your behavior as leader with a new team at the beginning of the cycle is critical. Teams that have initial briefings fare better than teams who receive no expectations at all. When you breathe new life into your team's structural shell, no matter how basic your cheer may be, you are helping your team to start pulling together.

Next, dive right in! It has been determined through study that teams which "plunge right in" do better than teams who "discuss strategy *ad nauseum*" at the start of work when nothing has yet been accomplished by the group. Members need experience before they can add useful input about how best to proceed together.

There may be some anxiety during the forming of a working group. Some members may feel that they don't know what to do. This is where Policies and Procedures or a Team Handbook can help to specify responsibilities.

2. STORMING

At the midpoint of the team's life cycle, there is a naturally occurring upheaval called storming. Expect it. At this point, mindfully reflect. What went wrong? What went right? How can plans can be revised and improved? Lower workload times can be an opportunity for conversations about the culture of the group.

Members now either get on board with the directives and plans, or they will quit. Be prepared for this, whether it is with a new volunteer board, practice team, or office initiative. **Storming represents a natural weeding out process.** You are better off with a team that is "all in" than a team with dissenters.

Openly discuss performance strategy at this point and help the team members to stay closely in touch with evolving chances for improvement. If you want a high-performing team, I suggest that you implement the "everyone talks to everyone" rule. There's no place for "passive-aggressive silent treatment" attitudes on a highly functioning team. During storming, personal matters that are entirely social in character need to be worked out.

There may be a strong tendency to defensively rationalize failure. Explore what can be learned from any given experience and brainstorm how systems can be improved. Switch into the learning mode. *Getting team members to discuss performance results is the first step toward success in the pursuit of excellence.* Eventually, the team will assume more responsibility for managing themselves. The team now becomes effective.

3. NORMING

Once life has been breathed into the team's structure and clarity has been established, the team will start to function on its own. The leader has helped the group go from being just a list of names on a roster to becoming a real, functioning, interactive social system—a team. The official tasks of the team have now been examined, assessed, and modified to establish each member's areas of responsibility.

The norms of behavior have also been tried out, and gradually revised and accepted. Goals, processes, and communication have been determined. The group is closer to ideal teamwork and unity.

4. PERFORMING

Team learning requires time and repetition to reach the highest level of performance. Team members will need to stay closely in touch with one another when working together.

The team owns their chosen performance strategies. They can discuss progress mindfully and efficiently. They can also choose to change or remove organizational constraints that may be restraining accomplishment.

You're now at the point of total quality management (TQM), which is a great place to be. The team now has knowledge and skill; they are aligned with reality. They are a high-performing collaborative team. They have a shared vision and strategies can be continuously improved. You're completely strategy-focused, and prepared for any eventuality.

THREE FUNCTIONS OF COACHING

A coach is someone who can give a correction
without causing resentment.
—John Wooden

It's back to the locker room, and the leader as coach has three functions: motivation, consultation, and education.

1. MOTIVATION

It's the first day of the month, and the game is about to get under way. Stay focused on what is to be achieved. Focus on goals for today, such as filling that one last opening in the office schedule, or collecting past-due accounts.

A motivational meeting, such as a morning huddle, is meant to "get down to business." These encounters result in a well-engaged team, ready to play as hard as possible. "Go team!"

3. CONSULTATION

It's halftime. Maybe it's the beginning of the third week of the month. How's your team doing? How far are you toward meeting your monthly goals? Do you need a revised game strategy or additional resources? Do some players need to raise their game? Do any changes need to be made?

The game strategy is reworked. The coach continues to offer words of encouragement. Corrections for enhanced team performance are made. Everyone is reminded that they need to be "all in." Everyone puts their hands, hearts, and minds together. It's one team, one score!

3. EDUCATION

The game is over, the month is over, or the year is over. It's time to evaluate what happened and plan for the future. The coach builds an agenda of learning, including what lessons have been gained to enhance team performance.

There is no one right way to implement the educational process for your team. But there is a wrong way. That is to implement a coaching style which is not your own. Take the John Wooden approach. During the game, stay quiet on the sidelines. Coaches who try to dictate the game from the sidelines might find themselves in as much trouble as the team. It is impossible to control every move that a team makes, whether in sports, a dental practice, or a dental society. Save educational efforts for after the contest, in the locker room, or on the practice field, such as during monthly or weekly meetings or annual advances.

What Coaches Do

In his book, *True North: Emerging Leader Edition*, author and former CEO Bill George describes what a coach does by the acronym **COACH:**

Care
Organize
Align
Challenge
Help.

Coaches understand their people. They care about each individual. They get people playing as a team and organize strength for the best performance possible. They inspire and unite their team around a common purpose. They challenge each person to do their best while reaching for the common goal. They solve team problems and celebrates successes.

What Coaches Don't Do

> *Good players take criticism.*
> *Great players crave criticism.*
> –Don Meyer

Great coaches are honest. I see this with my son's violin teacher as coach. A Juilliard graduate, he made his debut in Vienna at age fifteen. He was once the youngest player in the New York Philharmonic. He is a rock star. How did he get that way? He was brutally honest with himself about what he needed to improve. And, he is that way with his students. We love him for it. He is an awesome violin teacher. ***Great coaches don't hold back.***

Personally, I have learned a lot by doing many things "the hard way," through the experience of more than thirty years in dentistry. Some advice resonates with me, and some does not. I know one thing for sure; winning is not achieved by putting feelings above constructive criticism. ***Superficial harmony does not result in high performance.***

Team outcomes depend on the character of the members. Interpersonal conflicts, or the presence of dysfunctional behaviors, cannot be swept under the rug. These problems will continue to fester. Conflicts will be ever-present. What needs to be done is to look at the conditions that created the difficulties. Negativity or personality disorders may need to be addressed head-on.

Remove from your leadership mind that conflicts are necessarily bad for the group. Studies have shown that open communication, including conflicts, can actually promote group dynamics. Researchers have observed that well-performing teams exhibit moderate levels of conflict at the midpoint of team interaction. Conflicts can actually lead to better alignment with situational awareness.

Bottom line: a skilled coach, leader, or manager knows that sometimes it is best to let certain tensions smolder. Allowing negative interpersonal underbrush to burn out enables a healthy forest canopy of teamwork to grow.

The Power (or Lack of Power) of Committees

If you see a snake, just kill it—
don't appoint a committee on snakes.

–Ross Perot

I was once appointed to an orthodontic component committee. The first meeting didn't happen because the executive director didn't show up while we all waited. When we finally met, the committee chairwoman worked out on her treadmill while the committee talked. The meeting accomplished nothing. All I could think was, "What a waste of my time!"

It will be your job as leader of your dental office or president of your society to give assignments and to assign metrics, Key Performance Indicators (KPIs). There may be committees where you need to fill positions. Soon enough, you will discover who can and who cannot work as an effective member of a committee. You will also learn which committee is achieving goals and which is doing nothing. The results of a do-nothing committee will be zero. In your dental office, this will affect your decision about who should stay on any given project and who would best be replaced. As a leader in a nonprofit organization, you may have little to no control over a committee which is not performing. Any comment or reassignment attempt made may produce pushback and political protest.

THE STABILITY OF THE TEAM

In the dental office, team change is costly. When an employee is lost, you will inevitably need to train a new team member. Just when your team is perfect, someone may go out on family leave, another might move away, and yet another will retire. This is life. Stay positive and realize that this gives you the opportunity to build an even better team. It is difficult to replace a seasoned professional. So when you do have one on your team, treat them like gold.

In 2021 we lost such an office veteran. Jolene retired after being a registered dental assistant for thirty-eight years. While working at Gorczyca Orthodontics for twenty-four years, Jolene was my right-hand clinical coordinator. A person like this is irreplaceable. Filling her position required hiring two new team members! We devoted four full months to their training before Jolene left. I am happy to report that all has worked out well and Jolene still returns to work a day or two each month just for fun. As I write this book, Jolene has returned for two days to do Christmas deliveries to our referring dental offices. She loves her community and profession and it shows!

FINANCES

If you pay peanuts, you get monkeys.
–James Goldsmith

Dentists are, in general, fiscally conservative. They stay on top of their expenses, and collections. Dentists are faced with financial decisions on a daily basis, such as, "Should I hire another assistant?" Clear-eyed review of your office financial numbers will help you to make the best decisions for you and your practice.

Pay your team first. Treat them better than you treat yourself. You want the best team players that your money can buy. An excellent team player can do the work of three mediocre ones. You are better off with a small team where everyone is excellent than a huge team marked by mediocrity.

In orthodontics, our team costs range between twenty and twenty-five percent of collections. It is often said that an office is best served to have one team player for every $200,000 collected.

I often think: Collections = Profit + Expenses

Maximizing revenue and managing costs optimizes both team compensation and owner profit. Note that I speak of collections, not production. It is the money that you actually collect, your cash flow, which fuels your practice and compensates everyone who works there. Aim for patient and insurance payments to equal 100 percent of production.

ECONOMIES OF SCALE

One team in one location is a wonderful way to keep overhead costs down. It also simplifies life. Years ago, I worked in two offices. I worked Monday, Wednesday, and Friday in one location, then Tuesday, Thursday, and Saturday in a second. Once I paid off my new office, I settled down to that one location. A few weeks into the new work schedule, I thought to myself, "How did I ever survive with all that traveling and lack of consistency with two practices?" Life in one location is maximally efficient, and I've never looked back.

There are many benefits to having one convenient location besides reduced overhead costs. Other advantages include patient appointment availability, increased team employment hours, and consistency of care. I believe that sticking to a single address can help you to run a leaner, more competitive practice. Bigger is not always better when it comes to profitability.

Have a Plan, Then Roll Up Your Sleeves

If you can't describe what you are doing as a process,
you don't know what you're doing.
                                                    –W. Edwards Deming

Relentlessly implement your strategic plan. Your goals may be to improve cash flow or to buy equipment. They may include paying off an existing loan. Or, you may choose to optimize customer service or to achieve a certain number of new patients. Decide upon your aims, write them down, set up a system of progress measurement, and get to work. Have a process in place. Devise a plan.

In a group setting or dental society, the best thing that you can do is to get started on your own contribution. Everyone working together eliminates the "us versus them" mentality. Ask, "How can I help?" or state, "Let's work together." Get your own work done. No task is too small for the leader.

Chapter 15

HEALTH

Organizational health is
the single greatest competitive advantage in any business.
–Patrick Lencioni

C larity of communication is of upmost importance in the health of any organization. What are you trying to accomplish together? What does a job well done look like? Who is responsible for what? And, is there accountability of team members, following the rules of order?

In his book, *The Advantage: Why Organizational Health Trumps Everything Else in Business*, teamwork expert Patrick Lencioni describes organizational health as having five main components: Minimal politics, Minimal confusion, High morale, High productivity, Low turnover. He states that people in healthy organizations learn from one another, identify and address critical issues together, and recover quickly from mistakes.

Achieving organizational health will take clarity of messaging. There is no such thing as too much communication. Every policy, every meeting, and every communication should remind people of what is truly important to accomplish together. The single biggest factor determining whether an organization is going to be healthy is the genuine commitment and active involvement of the person in charge. A healthy organization of peer-to-peer accountability will need a leader who will confront difficult situations and hold people accountable herself. We call this "overcoming the 'Wuss' factor." The leader of the team will always be the ultimate arbiter of accountability and need to call someone on their behavior or performance when not up to the organizational standards.

THE TEAM MEETING

In another book, *Death by Meeting: A Leadership Fable about Solving the Most Painful Problem in Business,* Patrick Lencioni describes full team participation "like the lightning round on a game show." Everyone gets to talk. The agenda is flexible. The meeting is lively. Dare I say, exciting?

There can be no such thing as overcommunication. As leader, you will need to repeat the goals over and over again. It has been estimated that team members may need to hear objectives seven times before they understand and remember their importance. In the dental office, there are no surprises when it comes to achieving or not reaching the monthly goals. The end-of-month score is known by all. You either hit your metrics or you don't. These results will determine what your team will do next. Here is a sample business plan review meeting agenda for your dental office weekly team meeting:

WEEKLY BUSINESS PLAN REVIEW (BPR)

Doctor
>   Start the meeting

Treatment Coordinator
>   Number of new-patient exams completed month to date
>   Number of new-patient exams yet to be completed for the month
>   Number of new-patient treatments started month to date
>   Number of new patients total expected for the month
>   Conversion rate new patients/total exams, month to date, year to date

Public Relations Coordinator
>   Number of referral sources, year to date
>   Number of new patients started year to date
>   Referral sources

Records Coordinator
 Next week's schedule openings
Financial Coordinator
 Accounts receivable: 30, 60, 90 days
 Insurance receivables: 30, 60, 90 days
Doctor
 Projects report
 New initiatives
 Review of action items for the coming week
 Inspirational, educational, engagement, teamwork, exercise, or reading
 Grade meeting on a scale of 1-10, anonymous
 Meeting ends on time

In his book, *Traction: Get a Grip on Your Business*, Gino Wickman calls the weekly team meeting the moment of truth for accountability. Alan Mulally says that the only way that he knew how to operate was to have a weekly team meeting to review measurable goals.

Your meetings set your momentum. They keep your practice engine going. *It is the leader's job to set clear goals, to state who will do what, by when, and what the action item results of the meeting will be.* Start your meeting with the most pressing issue. That way, everyone's fresh attention and full energy will be focused on making this most important decision the top priority.

Everyone must have access to the reports for the team meeting. Review key performance indicators (KPIs) and anticipate weekly and end-of-month results. By working on the hourly, daily, and weekly plan, we know that, whatever the outcome, we have given it our very best.

Start and End Your Meeting on Time

Starting the meeting on time: it sounds easy. I assure you: it is not. There will be a straggler. No matter what, *start your meeting on time.* Starting on time shows respect for those present who made the effort to be there. It shows those who are late that it is *not* OK to be late. Those not present will miss out. Sooner or later, all members will make the extra effort to be ready on time.

Keep your eye on the time. If there are several things you need to cover, move on. Limit the rambling. When there are ten minutes left, announce the time, state, "We need to move on to complete all of today's business," or "The last topic will need an additional meeting." No matter what, *end the meeting on time.*

Wrap your meeting up with your "to-do" list. Who will do what? Each person can leave the meeting with at least one action item. You might want to go around the group one last time and ask each person one thing that they will accomplish this week. Then monitor progress. This strategy keeps the momentum of your team going.

Consider what type of "feelings" you want to result from your team meeting. Your job, as the leader, is for your team to leave the meeting feeling energized, focused, and inspired.

A LEVEL 10 MEETING

Improving meetings is not just an opportunity
to enhance performance of our companies.
It is also a way to positively impact the lives of our people.
–Patrick Lencioni

At the end of your meeting, ask your team to write a score between one and ten, ranging from "not so good" to "excellent." Emphasize that this is *your team score,* by asking the question, **"How did WE do?"** including the doctor, working together at this gathering. This score reflects *your* collective performance as a team.

It's not the economy, it's not the patients, it's not the pandemic, it is our own efforts which either hold us back or propel us forward. Encourage your team to be proactive. Avoid counterproductive attitudes such as:

Defending
Denying
Blaming
Excusing

194

Continue to focus on reality and what actions you can implement to reach your goals.

To achieve a Level 10 meeting, members are engaged in the discussion and not eating. Each has an opportunity to speak, and to feel good about themselves and their achievements. When an individual team member is upset or frustrated, they will give the meeting a lower score, maybe a seven or eight. If it was a great meeting, and they personally are doing well, they will score the meeting a ten. Pay attention to your team meeting scores as a barometer of teamwork and success.

CHEERLEADING

> *Cheerleading isn't big stuff,*
> *it's just a lot of little stuff every day.*
> –Richard DeVos

Language for making things happen includes: "Let's get that on the calendar now," or, "Let's do it!" A good leader or a good manager is like a conductor of a symphony orchestra. The leader listens to each instrument individually as the orchestra plays. The conductor might tone down the brass, ask for more woodwinds, or increase the tempo. By doing so, the maestro is bringing alive the desired perfect harmony.

Not having team meetings limits the possibilities of teamwork and collaboration. Don't hide behind the excuse, "I don't have enough time or money for a team meeting." This attitude is an abdication of teamwork and leadership and the chance for teamwork.

People in your organization do things well every day. They need affirmation for motivation, confidence, and self-esteem. A team meeting is a time to take pride in achievements and to offer thanks for what has been accomplished.

In his book, *Flip Your Focus: Igniting People, Profits and Performance Through Upside-Down Leadership*, consultant and author Bob Spiel writes, "Be a leader that your team will follow down a badger hole." I decided to share Bob's message with my staff at the next team meeting.

"No one can do what you do."

I reminded my team that I cannot answer the phone, that I don't print out the new-patient contracts, that I don't order the supplies, that I don't close out the end of day, and that I don't close out the end-of-the-month or the year-end final reports. *What each team member does is extremely important.* It makes a difference in the practice's success, in our patients' lives, in our community, and ultimately, in our own lives.

"You make a difference in the lives of your patients, your community, and your team."

Many people face personal daily challenges. They may feel lonely, unloved, stressed, or depressed. Coming into the dental office, receiving a warm welcome, tender loving care, and a fond farewell, or even just a "U R GREAT" Valentine heart may be the highlight of their day. Don't let this golden opportunity to make a difference in your patient's life pass unnoticed. Give special attention to maximizing your patient's office experience.

I will admit that the day I reviewed Bob Spiel's *Flip Your Focus* book with my team, we achieved an across-the-board level ten perfect score team meeting for the very first time. You want your team engaged, energized, and refreshed. Surprises and rewards help. Praise helps. Personal attention helps. A simple bag of Jelly Belly jelly beans sparks enthusiasm. Mix it up. Make your weekly team meeting something that everyone eagerly anticipates.

EFFICIENCY

Being productive gives people a sense
of satisfaction and fulfillment
that loafing never can.

–Zig Ziglar

The dental organizational chart is usually divided into two areas: front office (financial), and back office (clinical). These are the two basic operational units. Both departments have goals: to optimize efficiencies and economies of scale.

It is our leadership goal to maximize the output of our team. One outstanding, motivated, and hardworking team member can sometimes do the work of three mediocre individuals. It will be your leadership challenge to foster this type of maximized efficiency with an ideal team and management structure.

Have you ever noticed that on your lightest days you actually produce the most? There is a second aspect to efficiency, which is giving yourself time to accomplish what you set out to do. High-production days often happen when you have the latitude to begin immediately. Same-day starts depend on doctor time. Study your grid and consider using one chair as an unscheduled overflow chair. If you do, you will never be out of appointment times. Additional appointments can be worked in, seamlessly.

On non-patient days, ask whether a second receptionist is needed. Does the presence of the second receptionist produce results or "social loafing?" Should the second receptionist sit in a separate room to get her work done?

This thought came to me one Friday afternoon on a non-patient day. I was in my office calling patients on my thirty-plus days accounts receivable list. Meanwhile, my two receptionists were chatting up a storm. I thought to myself, "What's wrong with this picture?"

Now I have only one front-office team member, who also serves as my financial coordinator. When uninterrupted, she can accomplish more work. She often says, "Dr. Gorczyca, please don't come in on a non-patient day. I have work to do and I don't want to lose focus!" Now, with even greater efficiency, she is working off-site and out of state! All insurance and accounts receivables are up-to-date and our office efficiency has never been better! The phone is answered without a second ring, without the interference of a patient standing at the front desk. Studies done in hospitals have shown that off-site receptionists do indeed increase efficiency.

INEFFICIENCY

In a study of group size versus group productivity, psychologist Ivan Steiner found that the total amount of work produced continues to increase with group size, but at a decreased rate. Steiner states that larger groups never perform at their capable level of productivity. "Process losses" include motivational decrease, coordination problems, and other inefficiencies.

Neil Vidmar and J. Richard Hackman studied group size from two to seven members. Participants were asked if the group was too small or too large to complete the work. Analysis revealed that the optimum group size was 4.6 members (four to five).

Hackman states in his courses at the Harvard Business School that **an effective team cannot have more than six members.** A six-person team has fifteen possible pairings, but a seven-person team has twenty-one. The difference in how well the two sizes operate is noticeable. US Navy SEAL teams have six members.

Hackman once asked the executive director of a forty-member board of an art museum what they could accomplish. The director answered, "Not much other than financial contributions."

I once spent a weekend retreat with a board of approximately twenty members. They had a Friday night dinner during which leaders were watching a baseball game on their cell phones. Then came another Saturday night dinner. Sunday was time for new proposals. I submitted four proposals. They were the only four proposals submitted. My proposals were almost not accepted because "the submissions were not done correctly." I thought, "What are all these people doing here, except wasting time and money?" Two proposals were rejected. The other two were sent on to yet another board for yet another review at yet another meeting. I never saw the results of my proposals. My conclusion was that we had accomplished very little in three days. The lack of performance may have had less to do with individuals and more to do with the structure and size of the group.

A STRESS-FREE ENVIRONMENT

Laughter is not just laughter;
it's the most fundamental sign of safety and connection.
–Daniel Coyle

When everyone communicates openly about how shared systems of work are done, you will have a stress-free environment. As an example, staying on time enables you to deliver better customer service to your patients. Not only will patient satisfaction skyrocket, but you will have a calm doctor and a happy team. The gravest sin that the doctor commits is showing up late and running behind. Listen to your team. When they tap you on the shoulder as a signal, "We need to move on," wrap things up and stay on schedule.

When the doctor asks, "Where do I go next?" and the next patient is not ready, only then should the doctor return to their private office. If the assistant then comes to tell the doctor, "We're ready for you now," an unnecessary step has been created for the assistant. To speed up this process, my assistants use a shout-out: "Doctor, on your feet!" This phrase creates urgency and prevents unnecessary delays.

An outstanding team feels totally comfortable around each other. They enjoy each other's company and it shows. They value working for the doctor. Otherwise, perhaps staff should look for another job. **There are no dysfunctional behaviors on an ideal team.** There is only comfort and trust, with everyone bringing their whole self to work. The leader delivers praise throughout the day and radiates with delight over contributions of the team members. The environment is one of happiness, belonging, and co-elevation.

THREE CAUSES OF A STRESSED ENVIRONMENT

> *Dependability is not only about being there physically,*
> *but being there at your best.*
>
> –Coach K

1. LACK OF DEPENDABILITY

When a team member is not dependable, it puts a great stress on a small team. It is difficult to run an ideal dental practice while one person down. Make it a rule that everyone shows up every day at their best. Great team members are dependable.

In thirty-two years, I have never missed one day of work. Even though we have paid sick days in California, I am grateful that my team members rarely, if ever, are absent without forewarning. For time off, vacation, pregnancy, or family leave, we require a form to be submitted at least six weeks in advance. The request also lists the team member who will cover during the absence.

2. POOR RELATIONSHIPS

The biggest cause of stress in the dental office is two team members who do not get along. One might be giving the other "the silent treatment." Even grown male dentists give each other "the silent treatment," which is a dysfunctional behavior of passive aggression. It cannot be allowed in your office or in your volunteer society. If it occurs, pull both people aside, tell them that they need to communicate, or otherwise they both need to go.

3. STRAINED SCHEDULING

The third stress inducer is not being on time for patients. My scheduling coordinator does not allow random entries to mess up the daily flow. Being a registered dental assistant, she understands set-up time, clean-up time, doctor time, and the fact that the doctor can only be in one place at one time. She knows which appointments are best to schedule opposite each other, where the doctor needs to be during each procedure, and how many minutes of doctor time the intervention will take. She knows how to stagger procedures to produce the best working result for the team and doctor. We call this "doctor time scheduling."

Maximum production is when the doctor is busy at all times. The assistants wait with the patient ready to be seen by the doctor. The doctor is not waiting for the assistants or needing to be at three different locations simultaneously.

The biggest key to staying on time is finishing on time. Each assistant must know when the appointment is scheduled to end. If you have three procedures scheduled for a patient, and you are running late, you may decide to complete only two parts that day so that you can stay on time for all of your patients. You can reschedule the last procedure for the next appointment.

In orthodontics, this is easy to do. Each assistant is responsible for her own chair and schedule column. A patient may need a panoramic X-ray, banding of second molars, re-bond of a bracket, and a wire change during one visit. Should the patient arrive late, it is easy to complete banding at the next appointment. Perhaps this patient had a forty-minute slot and only twenty minutes are available. Complete what you can in twenty minutes. Stay on schedule.

Silos

> *The meeting of two personalities*
> *is like the contact of two chemical substances:*
> *if there is any reaction, both are transformed.*
> —Carl Gustav Jung

Groups of people tend to partition into silos of varying factions. You may have the front office, the back office, the university team, the study club team, the class of 1980 team, the society of older persons team. You cannot have a successful organization if you endorse exclusionary tactics, treating some people as the "in group" and others as second-class citizens. This is especially true of dental societies. This is why team meetings with everyone present, equal, and treated fairly with open-book management are so important. Your job will be to bring everyone in your organization together as one team.

Whether you are looking at a football team, a dental office team, or a society, ask, "Is this one team, or two different teams?"

Should you find yourself in a situation where there is a "meeting after the meeting," this is not a good sign. Watch out for someone uncharacteristically not speaking up during the meeting. Someone may be running a subversive group within the organization. Non-communicators will work to privately push their own agenda. Perhaps someone is planning a walk out, a takeover, or anarchy. Get the issue out in the open. Ask, "What's up?" Whatever it is, you need to talk about it. Worse yet, beware of private chats during a Zoom meeting or texting between attendees of an in-person gathering.

One CEO of a start-up organization created a "must always do" norm for his board. Each member was assigned responsibility for staying closely in touch with each of the other officers. Before every task force meeting, each person was expected to speak to all of the other team members individually. You may want to put this practice in place for your office and for your volunteer dental society. Communication is the antidote to silos.

If you, as the leader, are making decisions about the direction of your office or volunteer organization and someone has a concern, I would expect that person would feel free to speak up. Calmly back up your position with data. Remember, the numbers set you free. Stay focused on your common goals. Make decisions through dialog, and when appropriate, with a vote.

An Apology

> *Never ruin an apology with an excuse.*
> –Benjamin Franklin

Years ago, the University of North Carolina residents visited my practice on a one-week tour of Northern California. When I discussed employee turnover with the young doctors, I told them that when they lose a team member, to remember that everyone is replaceable and move on. What I meant by the statement was, **have the courage to find a new team member quickly and don't dwell on the past.** From the perspective of a practice owner, that is what we need to do. I wanted the residents to understand this concept that they will face in their careers, to be strong, and take action.

The team member sitting at the front desk at that moment took the statement personally. That was not my intention. The comment didn't apply to her or anyone in my practice. I was remembering how I felt when I was first confronted with replacing a valued team member who had moved on. The fact is, even the doctor is replaceable. I tell my team often, should something happen to me, there will be a new orthodontist in the office within one week.

Everyone tends to internalize discussions. Funny thing, this team member waited seven years to tell me that this bothered her! I promptly apologized. Ask the question, "Is anything bothering you?" Maybe you will be able to clear the air faster that way. Part of success is not taking things too personally.

I remember vividly my first day at the Harvard School of Dental Medicine in a class at Harvard Medical School. The professor stated, "All of you are replaceable. What you have done in the past doesn't matter. All that matters is what you do here now." I totally understood this statement and it didn't upset me. Success is rooted in the reality of hard work and results. Ego is not part of it. However, there are some people who do not appreciate the story's point, which is to be humble and be prepared to apologize when necessary.

We all see and feel things through our own experiential lenses. We all see things from the inside out. We see the world, how we are conditioned to see it.

One thing that I have learned during the time of writing this book and studying leadership and teamwork, is that people today, perhaps affected by the social isolation of the pandemic, or frequent Zoom meetings, have become exceedingly sensitive and emotionally charged. There is no harm in an apology. It tells the other person, "I hear you." By doing so, you give unconditional love. Gentleness can only be expected from the strong. Choose to be strong and apologize.

ECONOMIES OF SCALE

You will spend your entire career fine-tuning your team, schedule, and salary for ideal work-life balance. You might call this "maximizing happiness." In the area of team size, economies of scale may not work.

As noted above, *research has shown that the ideal team size is between four and five.* A dentist has total discretion about this issue. Sometimes managers or doctors may feel that the team is too small to accomplish their work. Author J. Richard Hackman argues that it is far more common and dangerous to overstaff. If your dental office team costs are high, start looking at performance.

Years ago, I hired a new receptionist who was to function as financial coordinator. I called her previous employer and asked, "Would you rehire her?" The doctor stated, "Yes, *but...*" When you hear the *but*, run. She asked if she could have a week vacation before starting her first day of work. Soon afterwards, her "mother had heart problems." Then, her "daughter needed an operation." Next, she herself "had pneumonia." Then came family car accidents. One day, I was left with no one to cover the front desk. I was forced to hire an additional receptionist. Now I had two "C" players on my team instead of one "A" player. This was a costly mistake.

The "frequently missing" employee finally quit. The receptionist without previous dental experience decided that she did not want to work long hours. So, these two were replaced with one A+ player who was able to complete three times the work. Although her salary was higher, the net result was a cost savings. The team got smaller, yet it became more productive.

Systems of a Healthy High-Performance Team

Success is the maximum utilization of the ability you have.
–Zig Ziglar

What can we learn from an airline crew? This is perhaps the highest performing team in the business world. A flight crew comes together as a new team for every flight. They start prepared. They know the handbook rules. They have excellent attitudes and work ethics. They work together as a team seamlessly. The pilot briefs the team. They're ready to go. The crew performs to perfection. They have to. You put your life in their hands whenever you fly.

What guarantees such exceptional leadership and teamwork? Discipline of systems. A flight crew's handbook is explicitly clear. Cooperation and understanding must be 100 percent.

The pilot and co-pilot go down the checklist. Not only do they have a handbook, but they have a culture of preparedness.

There is no time for "forming, storming, norming, and performing" with a flight crew. They start already normed, and performing flawlessly every time.

We can do the same in our dental societies and practices. All it takes is attention to detail and discipline. When the leader begins his/her briefing with the Team Handbook, Policies and Procedures, Bylaws, and/ or documented management systems as their foundation, they are not starting from ground zero every time. Effective teamwork does not just happen—it takes effort and execution by everyone on the team, especially the leader.

Can your new team member jump right in and do what needs to be done? Or do you go through "forming, storming" phases every time? If we are to optimize teamwork in dentistry, we need to pay close attention to well-organized, real-world organizations and the best-practice systems that make them work.

Chapter 16

GOALS

Goals transform a random walk into a chase.
                    –Mihaly Csikszentmihalyi

A nswer these questions: "What does a win look like for us?" and, "What does a loss look like?" The wonderful thing is, when you have a business plan that is known by all, everyone on the team knows a win. The team has a goal.

As compared to sports leagues, in your dental office you basically compete against yourself. How successful do you want to be? How hard are you willing to work? And, do you accept ownership and accountability for your results?

Winning usually has a numerical value. It could be production, collections, or conversion rate. It could be profitability, or saving enough money to go on a trip. It might be getting accounts receivables to zero. Whatever winning means to you, set attainable goals and work on them together. This is what makes teamwork fun.

SMART GOALS

SMART stands for Specific, Measurable, Achievable, Realistic, and Time-Bound goals. Here is an example of a SMART goal.

At the beginning of 2021, I decided to set a team goal of reaching forty-two new-patient exams per month. I set this specific goal because I knew that with our conversion rate at that time, we would certainly reach our new-start goal at this number. Broken down, this goal could easily be achieved with four new exams per day worked; that would only be two exams in the morning, and two exams in the afternoon. It was realistic that we could attain this milestone if we increased our new-exam marketing by twenty-five percent. Lastly, as with any new project, the plan was to assess the metrics after ninety days.

Well-stated goals are precise, positive, and written down. Let's rename them SMARTER goals: Specific, Measurable, Attainable, Results-Oriented, Trackable, Ethical, and Recorded.

From this overall goal of four new exams per day, the treatment coordinator could aim to start one of the new exams on the same day. That's only a twenty-five percent conversion rate, which is totally doable. The records coordinator could do two new records per day, also doable. We would repeat this program on a daily basis and check our results each week and at the end of the month.

The performance goals of your practice should be clear: new-patient exams each month; new cases started; schedule for the following week filled; inventory restocked; referring dentists visited and well-cared for; marketing for next month set; all referral sources producing; accounts receivables heading toward zero; insurance receivables headed toward zero; collections and production moving upward.

You must together with your staff work on these goals. Although any given KPI may be assigned to one person, all goals belong to the whole team. Graphs and charts can visually display "How are we doing?" It's one team, one score. It's that easy. It can also be fun.

Got Goals?

The way to get started is to quit talking and begin doing.
–Walt Disney

Most people have goals. What everyone does not have are the intentions and an action plan as to how they will achieve those goals. As an example, if I need to improve progress in the office, I will call my missed exams a second time that month in an effort to fill an open exam slot. I will contact additional referring dental offices and make arrangements to discuss patient cases with the dentists. I will hand out a few more "Refer a Friend" cards to my existing patients. Stated another way, what is your overreaching *strategy* and specific *tactics* to making your goals a reality?

Missed exams are the low-hanging fruit in the dental office production efforts. The follow-up calls cost you nothing. If you make the calls, you can probably schedule two more exams right now and possibly see them today or tomorrow.

Many new patients come directly from existing patients. In an effort to increase patient-referred exams, you can send a mass email to every family in your database today. It's a reminder that you're there to help with their dental needs. By keeping in touch, and being top of mind with your past, present, and future patients, you will schedule more exams.

You can also give out "Refer a Friend" cards or other personalized practice items to your existing patients. I also ask the parents, friends, and family who physically come into my office with my patients if they would be interested in scheduling an exam. You would be pleasantly surprised how many say yes.

General dentists refer a lot of patients to specialists for new-patient exams. They usually send a referral card. These cards can be reviewed to make sure that every referral has scheduled an exam. If not, the dentist as the leader can personally call the new patient to boost success rates of exam scheduling and follow-through. Dentists can also give these referral cards to specialists and receive new patients in return when specialty exams see new patients in need of a general dentist.

One of my favorite activities is taking dentists out to lunch and going over some orthodontic cases. I usually get the response, "Oh, I just saw a patient with that problem this week," which leads to more referrals. To replicate that outcome, you can pick up the phone today and call ten offices to invite doctors out to lunch at their earliest convenience.

These actions are key tactics to increase new-patient exams and cost only time and effort. The team can act on all of these items, but if I truly want something done now, I lead by example, and do it myself.

If a serious surge in new-patient exams is necessary, I might pull out the heavy artillery and order up some Google ads. The agency I use for this initiative is PostcardMania. Find them at www.PostcardMania.com. If I need an increase in new-patient exams, I would increase my last order by ten percent.

Intentions are justifications for actions behind your deeds. If you intend to achieve your specific goals, your deeds will follow. For these and more marketing tips, check out my book on Amazon: *It All Starts with Marketing: 201 Marketing Tips for Growing a Dental Practice.*

INDIVIDUAL GOALS

> *Success is steady progress toward one's personal goals.*
> –Jim Rohn

I once saw Steffi Graf play in a tournament in Indian Wells, California. She was the number-one women's tennis player in the world at that time. She was unbeatable. The reason that I made the long day trip was that I wanted to see her feet in action. Steffi Graf had the fastest feet in tennis. Her feet never stopped moving, like those of a prize fighter. As a tennis player myself trying to improve my game, I knew how hard this was to do. It's akin to jumping rope continuously for over forty minutes. I watched in awe as she beat her opponent 6-2, 6-0. I wondered, "What keeps this champion going?"

Later in an interview, I heard her answer. "My goal is always to keep trying to get better. If I play an opponent, and I've played them before, I try for a better score with a faster time. If I beat them last time in fifty-five minutes, this time I go for forty-five!"

Champions have goals. They are always looking to improve. Here lies the compelling reason to assign KPIs to team members. KPIs give everyone an individual goal and the opportunity to become a champion. It provides something unique to work on. Great leaders help their team members understand how they directly impact the company's success through their own personal efforts. Achieved KPI scores are concrete evidence of that aspiration.

A Growth Mindset

> *Effective people are not problem-minded;*
> *they're opportunity-minded.*
> *They feed opportunities and starve problems.*
> –Stephen R. Covey

For someone to feel excited about the future, that person must have the ability to shape it. This is the essence of empowerment. Ask your team the question, **"What would our office have to do for you to wake up every morning excited about coming to work?"** By answering this query, we are collaborating on our common vision, one for which the team feels ownership and which motivates to shape their own destiny. knowing that together, we can get there.

Challenge each person on your team to state one thing that they can do today, to make their vision for their ideal future a reality. You can write each person's response down on a whiteboard and save it for the next meeting. Now, you have taken the first step toward achieving this goal. Managing change combines orienting others in a forward-facing direction and fostering a mindset for growth.

THREE PERSONAL GROWTH STATEMENTS

Reward the behavior you want repeated.
–Larry Winget

Acknowledge improvement. Give rewards, praise, and special recognition for loyalty and professional growth. Provide time and attention for annual reviews. Co-elevate each other. Liberate your team by giving them the freedom they need to raise their standard of excellence. A positive culture enables staff to be creative, take risks, and strive toward continuous improvement.

To help your team members achieve their potential, have them complete the following three statements:

1. *My untapped talents are* _____.
2. *If I had the freedom to fail, I would* _____ *to make this office better.*
3. *I can best contribute to practice growth by* _____.

Appreciate and maximize each employee's talents. A team which grows together stays together. By fostering professional development, the entire office will reap the rewards.

OPENING A PRACTICE

When I was thirty-four years old, my mother sat across from me at my apartment kitchen table. She had flown out to California from Massachusetts to catch up on how I was doing. I told her I was perfectly happy with my life and my surroundings and having a great time.

With a pensive look, she gazed into my eyes, and with an air of disbelief, and some disappointment, she held out her hands toward me to ask:

"Don't you have any long-term goals?"

This question cut like a knife. Of course, I had long-term goals! I had just finished eleven years of professional school and I was an orthodontist! But that was in the past. This was now. What were my goals now?

She followed the question with the statement, "Your father and I didn't work this hard to put you through school to see you living in this apartment." I knew that day that I needed to open my own practice to fulfill my life goals. The rest is history. I opened my practice from scratch that year.

Perhaps you need to hear these words and think these same thoughts to motivate yourself. Do you need to open or buy your own practice? What are you waiting for? Perhaps you need a gentle push from someone who loves you or from this book or a motivational speaker for you to live your best dental life. Opening a practice is a decision that I have never regretted. It can be the same for you.

WORKING TOGETHER TO ACHIEVE GOALS

What you get by achieving your goals is not as important
as what you become by achieving your goals.
–Zig Ziglar

Ask the question, "What do we need to do to create a business that's going to grow?" Keep asking that question. Do you need to ramp up your efforts? Go through your entire scorecard and give an accurate account of progress. Trust the process of getting things out in the open. Once data are presented through open-book management, you can start improving systems to reach your goals.

Everyone on the team helps to achieve the goals, from the person who answers the phone, to the person who cleans the dental instruments, to the dentist/owner. Everyone on the team who does the day-in, day-out work of the office contributes to team performance. Celebrate every win as a team as well.

Everyone needs encouragement, from the star player to the middle performers, to the person who may be experiencing a struggle to get the work done, to the doctor. Yes, that's right. Even the doctor needs constructive feedback and support! No matter what the team position, everyone must be valued for their contribution.

Chapter 17

CROSS-TRAINING

I aimed to have the USS Benfold *four deep in people*
who could handle every job onboard.
–Captain D. Michael Abrashoff

C ross-training involves preparing each team member, who already has a primary job, to perform additional work functions. Cross-training has many organizational benefits. When team members learn from one another, not only does this build understanding and connectedness, but it also expands the total pool of talent. Process gains are made when everyone in the office has a vast array of skills and knowledge.

EIGHT BENEFITS OF CROSS-TRAINING

Cross-training builds respect for, and understanding of each team member's tasks and unique daily challenges. Cross-training can be a great team-building exercise, offering an opportunity for future promotion within your organization as employees continue to develop their talents and skills. Here are eight benefits of cross-training:

1. *Strengthens relationships and understanding of the team*
2. *Improves communication*
3. *Grows knowledge and skill*

4. *Reduces boredom*
5. *Protects the office against absence or change*
6. *Increases flexibility*
7. *Improves efficiency*
8. *Creates opportunity for promotion*

TWO QUESTIONS FOR A CROSS-TRAINED TEAM

1. "DO YOU NEED HELP?"

When staff feel overwhelmed, they need to ask for help. By doing so, the shared task can be completed more quickly and easily.

In my HR book, *"Beyond the Morning Huddle,"* I describe a situation where, when asked, an employee told her doctor that all of the treatment plan letters are completed. Upon her resignation, the dentist discovered a stack of uncompleted letters still needing to be written. The doctor immediately hired a transcriptionist who had all letters completed within two weeks.

This completion process could have happened earlier if the doctor had known the truth. In such circumstances, the doctor wonders, "Why didn't this team member ask for help?" Perhaps she did not know that assistance would be readily available, perhaps she was embarrassed that her work was not done, perhaps she thought that she could somehow catch up, or perhaps she feared that telling the truth would jeopardize her job. Asking, "Do you need help?" would have prevented this situation from occurring.

2. "WOULD YOU LIKE ME TO HELP YOU?"

It needs to be emphasized during cross-training sessions that offering comes before starting to help. The goal is respectful assistance, not escalation of tension by making someone feel uncomfortable. If it is easier for the person to complete the task themselves, they will tell you so. This applies not only to teammates, but also for the doctor. If you ask, "Would you like me to help with that?" accept the answer that you received, even if it is a decline.

During 360 annual reviews, one team member wrote, "Make sure you ask every team member for help, not just one person." How lucky am I? Everyone on my team wants to pitch in! Your team should be there to assist you. Therefore, get comfortable saying, "Can you help me?" That's why you hired dental "assistants" in the first place!

BACKUP

There is no downside to cross-training. Front-desk personnel cross-training guards against embezzlement by having multiple eyes on contracts, write-offs, and collections. With cross-training, you will never be "held hostage" by just one person knowing how to do a certain job, and no one else to fill in.

As a practical example, what do you do if your treatment coordinator goes on a two-week vacation? With cross-training, someone else will be able fill in. It is possible the doctor could do the exams alone and someone else could help the doctor by taking notes and presenting the financial arrangements.

Doctors can and should be prepared to discuss payment. The conversation goes like this:

"The fee for this service is $X. You can make a down payment of $Y, which will leave you with a monthly payment of $Z, over N months. Does that work for you? Great! Let's get started!"

You did it! You closed the deal! This conversation takes approximately thirty seconds. The financial coordinator can then get the contract ready and have the patient or family sign the paperwork needed to begin with treatment.

THE TRUCK TEST

Could your team pass "the truck test?" It goes like this: if one of your team members got hit by a truck, can other members step in and immediately do the job with minimal disruption?

For a leader, the most common "what-if" scenario involves losing people. With effective cross-training, you are guaranteed to always have backup to get a job done. This preparation gives the leader peace of mind and prevents the need to scramble for a new team member quickly. To avoid shortages of workers, always keep resumes on file even if you do not presently have a job opening. The same practice also applies to board members in volunteer organizations.

My Job

You can't become a good general
if you haven't learned to take orders from a sergeant.
–Napoleon Bonaparte

En route to becoming CEO of the muti-billion-dollar company Xerox, Ursula Burns had done most of the major jobs in her twenty-eight years at the company where she once starting as an intern. It is not surprising that she was elevated to the C-suite as she had walked the walk instead of talking the talk.

I'm not a fan of job descriptions, although I've used them when necessary. I've often told my team members, "Your job is to do whatever needs to be done in the office." I never want to hear the words ‚"That's not my job." Even the CEO of Disneyland, Michael Eisner, was often seen picking up garbage.

I have a small team that produces great results. Everyone pitches in and helps wherever assistance is needed. You can often find my financial coordinator cleaning instruments at the end of the day. My back-office dental assistant calls pending patients who speak Spanish. My clinical coordinator delivers thank-you gifts to referring doctors. My records coordinator and my clinical assistant also know how to make clear aligners in the lab. I never hesitate to make patient calls myself. With cross-training, no one is ever stressed or bored. There's always something to do. Through cross-training, team members are fulfilled by being able to reach their full potential.

On a team, every job can be your job. You're there to help out however you can, until all the work is done. Job descriptions in themselves will not motivate a person to work. Job descriptions are default "low bars" that, at best, only serve to document an underachiever's shortcomings.

There is no need in a busy dental office for one person to sit idle in the corner waiting for the phone to ring. The constant availability of new challenges is one of the elements of business that makes it so exhilarating.

Now make a chart. Across the top, write each team member's name and their primary job. Under their name, list the next person to cover in their absence, then the next, and the next, until you run out of team members to add to the column and the doctor has to cover. Start cross-training in this order.

When team members understand everyone's work, it is easier to become a self-managing team. Team members can help each other first, without automatically involving the doctor. I once asked at the team meeting, *"Does anyone feel that I am holding them back from reaching their true growth potential?"* That day we discussed opportunities for future continuing education that would catalyze individual and group advancement.

On a board, an example of self-management might be someone who knows more about the task than the person assigned to do the job. Sharing experience will be beneficial for everyone on the team. Take advantage of expertise.

One of the most common missed opportunities on volunteer boards is the inappropriate deference given to a member's background of previous positions held, behavioral style, or verbal dominance, rather than what a person actually contributes and accomplishes. This wastes a precious commodity—the talents of all other members. Lack of participation can become extremely discouraging for those who are most actively engaged in the group effort. They might view others as "loafers." Don't let this be the case in your organization. Pay attention to the doers. Tell the talkers, "Let's move on" and get them working on a project of their own.

Connect Your Team by Analysis

When holding the weekly BPR (business plan review) meeting, start with printed reports of practice metrics. You need to work together to improve these lead measures. Progress is daily and gradual. Every night before leaving the office, the day sheet should be reviewed. This is how great teams stay on course, by checking the team score. There is satisfaction in seeing your outcomes continuously rising and taking the actions necessary to keep that score high.

Consider mapping the patient experience of care in your dental office as lanes of a pool. In his book, *The Frontline CEO: Turn Employees into Decision Makers Who Innovate Solutions, Win Customers, and Boost Profits,* former CEO and management consultant Eric Strafel uses a figure called "The Olympic Pool Diagram" to demonstrate how each team member contributes to success by what they accomplish in their lane. The order of lanes indicates handoffs. As you work left to right from the initial phone call to the final appointment, each team member will realize the value of their service. This visual shows that everyone's role is interconnected.

With this technique, you might also spot inefficiencies, wastes, or pinch points, where team members are stuck waiting for another team member to complete their job. When you see such a speed bump, you can redeploy resources to eliminate it to keep moving things along more efficiently.

Reviewing this process with my own team, I learned that we needed a curing light at each chair so as to not waste chair time waiting for a light. Our goal is a seamless delivery process of care. Sharing equipment back and forth is one area where time can be conserved and quality of patient care improved. Another quality improvement would be sharpening instruments or using new burs for more efficient treatment. Attention to these small details saves time and money.

SYSTEMS

> *Systems run the business and people run the systems.*
> –Michael E. Gerber

Once you have your patient experience mapped, actions can be aggregated into a systems management playbook. Creating this book can be another team project. The Ritz Carlton's MR. BIV Handbook documents over one thousand customer service mishaps and how to prevent them. MR. BIV stands for Mistakes, Rework, Breakdowns, Inefficiencies, and Variations. MR. BIV is described in my book, *At Your Service: 5-Star Customer Care for a Successful Dental Practice.*

Reviewing your systems is the process that all leaders and teams devoted to customer service master. Your goal is to prevent mishaps. Creating your own book of operational systems will be of priceless value to your organization.

Once you have your systems in place, input can be adjusted. Maybe you need more days worked, additional assistants, or ramped-up marketing. This way of thinking ensures that you stay on track, maintain your momentum, and *hold yourself accountable* to achieve your goals.

Chapter 18

SOLUTIONS

Turn justified complaints into positive solutions.
–Jon Gordon

M y dad told me, "In life, always expect the unexpected." As a result, when the unexpected happens, I am never surprised. I deal with it as part of life. I never asked the question, "Why me?"

Who would have predicted the financial downturn of 2008, the COVID pandemic, or an employee's unpredictable behavior? As long as we practice dentistry, unforeseen circumstances will arise and dentists, as leaders, will need to deal with them.

When the unexpected occurs, whining is not a plan. Fear is not an option. Withdrawal is not an appropriate response. Taking action is the only way forward. Start with yourself. Ask, "What did I do, or not do, to contribute to this situation?" Fix that first. Then, come up with a solution. Adjust your plan for success.

The 90-Day Turnaround

Your positive energy and vision
must be greater than anyone's and everyone's negativity.
Your certainty must be greater than everyone's doubt.

–Jon Gordon

There will come a time when something will intensely challenge you. Efforts which have always worked will not deliver the desired results. You evaluate the situation, but you can't determine the cause. It is then that you will need to bring in a coach.

When you have a lump on your back that you cannot see, the discovery will always surprise you. In the office, it could be a team member not doing their job, or it could be some type of internal sabotage to your practice or organization. These things exist, and it is extremely important that you as a practice owner smoke them out quickly.

When writing my book, *Beyond the Morning Huddle, Human Resource Management for a Successful Dental Practice,* I had the opportunity to work with David Harris, CEO of Prosperident, on chapters of dealing with embezzlement and sabotage. Dysfunctional behaviors were reviewed by psychologist and leadership coach Wayne Pernell. The book was reviewed by attorney Art Curley. Through this process, my understanding of how frequently dentists are bullied, cheated, taken advantage of, and disrespected to the point where their own physical lives could be in danger, changed my understanding of dental practice management and organizational leadership forever.

It is best to accept the realities of business ownership and organizational leadership. Be prepared to deal with difficulty. I have found through my own experiences, with my coach, Aimee Nevens of Fortune Management, that once you do address difficult situations and take action, any unwanted situation can be resolved within ninety days.

Emotional Intelligence

*Emotional intelligence emerges as a much stronger predictor of who
will be most successful, because it is how
we handle ourselves in relationships
that determines how well we do once we are in a given job.*
                                                    –Daniel Goleman

Self-control is emotional intelligence and describes how we handle ourselves in times of high stress. This is especially challenging if you are the
leader. Everyone is watching you. They are looking for weaknesses and
how you will react in tough situations. The team needs reassurance that
following you is the right decision. You want your behaviors to produce
the answer "yes."

I will always remember my toughest work day, the day of the 9/11
attack. After seeing the Twin Towers being hit on TV, I drove myself to
work. When I arrived, no one was talking. I said, "It's business as usual.
Everything is going to be alright." Inside, I was thinking, "Is someone
going to fly a plane into our three-story building today?" Together, we
channeled our courage. We kept calm and carried on.

We've all heard the advice that when a problem arises, you should
"sleep on it." Take time to calm down and think about it. Don't fly off the
handle, or have a panic attack, or an emotional breakdown.

Next time you find yourself in a difficult situation, take a deep breath.
Maintain composure and adopt a problem-solving stance. There will
always be stressors. It is how you deal with stress that counts.

The 360-Degree Review

Annual reviews recap what each team member is doing well, as well
as areas for improvement. The 360-degree review in the dental office
include suggestions from all staff and the doctor. This gives everyone the
opportunity to share what another team member does well, what they
like about that person, and what could be improved. This can be a very
positive experience.

If five team members make the same comment, the employee will take this constructive criticism very seriously. Peer influence or "peer pressure" is the most powerful force for change. No one wants to let down the team.

Everyone can be reviewed on the same day, including the doctor. Reviews should not be rushed. I like to do these yearly reviews on the last day of a month, preferably before a weekend or vacation.

It is helpful to have the doctor paired with an assigned HR team member or an outside consultant to do the reviews. Working together makes the process complete and more professional. A self-evaluation is also included. Everyone hears that their hard work and commitment are appreciated. Suggestions for growth are given for the coming year. Overall, it is an extremely positive and valuable experience for all. Performance Appraisal forms can be obtained from HRDirect.com. A careful and structured approach to reviews results in personal and professional growth that fosters a thriving office environment.

CASE 16: THE SURPRISE

Amy dropped her resume at her dentist's office as she was looking for a job while continuing her college studies at night. She was hired as a receptionist. Amy's work was sound. There was just one problem. At a weekly team meeting, when money was discussed, Amy verbally blew up like a firecracker. She started attacking others with loud, disrespectful discourse. Shocked by the out-of-control behavior, the doctor declared, "This meeting is over. Please clock out and come back at 1:30 p.m."

Knowing there was an emotional problem beyond her control, the doctor called her coach. She explained that her leadership had failed to produce expected standards of behavior and that she needed help. The coach then entered the team meetings to work on communication skills. For a short time, all was well. Then came the annual performance reviews, which were filled out by the doctor and reviewed by the coach. Team members also did self-evaluations and reviewed the doctor. Everyone had done well and raises were planned. That day, the doctor offered a few words of gratitude before the start of the reviews. It was meant to be a happy day of shared success.

The doctor and coach proceeded with Amy's review. All of the initial categories were marked "very good." Then they got to the category of "Interpersonal Relations," which was rated "80% good." The doctor read one sentence of suggested improvement, "Please don't give the doctor a hard time."

Once again, Amy had an uncontrolled emotional outburst, shouting accusations, including, "I know how to run this practice better than you do!"

The doctor once again stopped the meeting, saying, "Let's take a break. Let's resume after lunch." She could not allow this type of behavior to continue. She stated that perhaps the review could be completed after lunch with the team HR representative and the coach instead of with herself.

The coach stated that the situation was much worse than originally described. After lunch, the coach and HR team member finished the review. The review lasted two more hours. The coach and HR team member listened, questioned, and documented the continued outrage, trying to reason and seeking to understand. Amy got her raise. At this difficult day's end, the coach stated, "We've got a serious problem on our hands." The doctor noted that she preferred that team members resign rather than be dismissed. It was decided to let the situation play out.

The next day, Amy was back in the office. She appeared fine and completed the day's work well. At closing, Amy came to the doctor's private office and stated, "My father wants to speak to you on the phone."

The doctor replied, "No. I am not going to speak to your father on the phone. Amy, you are an adult."

Within thirty seconds, a very large, angry man appeared in the doorway of the doctor's private office. "DO YOU KNOW WHO I AM?" he yelled.

The doctor replied, "No sir, I do not know who you are."

"YOU HAVE NO RIGHT CRITICIZING MY BUSINESS!"

The doctor replied, "Sir, I know nothing about your business." She stood from her desk and called out to her assistant in the clinic as she squeezed out her office door past the man. The doctor told the assistant, "I'll be right back," and quickly exited the back door to her office. She entered her neighbor's dental office and locked the door behind her. She called the police.

One half-hour later, the police escorted the man and the assistant out of the building. When the doctor returned to her private office, the receptionist's resignation was on her desk. The doctor promptly changed all the locks on her office doors and reset security codes on the alarm system.

Solution:

Be aware that as dentists, we deal with a vast array of personality types and their families. As with any situation, should you feel that you are unsafe, you must protect yourself.

Whether it be verbal abuse, threats, feelings of embezzlement or sabotage, or blatant disrespect, these undesirable actions must be identified, called out, and terminated. Otherwise, they will continue to resurface as serious aggressions. Do not pretend that they don't exist. Take immediate action. Better safe than sorry.

RED FLAG

Failure isn't the end of the road.
It's a big red flag saying to you,
"Wrong way. Turn around."
—Oprah Winfrey

Should a discussion get too uncomfortable, call out "red flag," the equivalent to "time-out." It may be best at times to give the conversation or the meeting a rest. Sometimes it is prudent to step back, observe behavior, and contemplate a new course of action.

There will be times when you, as the leader, may need to say, "Let's sleep on this issue until next time." You want to cultivate a culture of trust, empowerment, and feedback that inspires everyone to pull together toward a common solution. Discretion is sometimes the better part of valor, and taking a deep breath is sometimes the best course of action. Be decisive as a leader to maintain a positive co-elevating environment.

FEEDBACK

> *Being vulnerable together is the only way*
> *a team can become invulnerable.*
> –Daniel Coyle

The US Navy SEALs are the greatest teamwork show on earth. They need to be. They are fighting together in life-or-death situations. Here, the leader is part of the team. It can be the same in your dental practice.

How can a dental office develop this hive mentality of elite teamwork? We can do this by creating the conditions that make this type of cohesiveness possible. Encourage problem-solving. Ask questions. Your team members need to speak up and feel comfortable doing so. Foster this behavior of group discussion.

To emphasize the importance of open communication and your own receptivity to feedback, tell your team:

"We might have a serious problem with a patient, a procedure, a referring doctor, or a team member. When this happens, are you going to tell me about it? Or, are you going to sit there quietly and let me put our practice and all of us at risk?"

Always speak with candor. This is why I love my son's weekly violin lessons. It's an exercise in emotional intelligence and the ability to receive candid feedback. This is an important skill that helps to ensure never-ending improvement and success in life.

Great violin teachers are totally honest. They don't second guess: "Will this comment hurt my student's feelings?" Nothing is sugar-coated. Progress is the goal, note by note, measure by measure. Detailed, focused feedback translates into incremental improvement.

My team knows that I am limited when it comes to information technology. I bought my first personal computer when I was thirty years old. I ask for reports, and when necessary, I hire consultants to review the data generated by my office computer software.

A group understanding of any given team member's shortcomings allows for outstanding teamwork. Highly charged and maybe even awkward interactions may seem like the opposite of team cooperation but I assure you, they are not. Feedback is best when extremely honest. This is candor at its finest.

It is when vulnerabilities are shared that the behaviors necessary for teamwork and cooperation are generated. When no one is holding back from the conversation, you know that all truly want what is best.

Take time to ask your own staff as well as your dental colleagues, *"What have you done that worked exceptionally well? What do you wish that you had done differently?"*

My dental practice management books document over thirty years of receiving feedback. There is a difference between owning a dental practice and working as a dental coach or consultant. As the owner, you deal with whatever comes your way, which translates into hard-earned experience. Learn as much as you can from others' experiences, such as by reading this book and my other books. If you are faced with a challenge, it is likely that others have also encountered a similar circumstance and you can benefit by seeking out their feedback, expertise, and best-practice guidance.

AFTER-ACTION REVIEW

The US Navy SEALs have a system of after-action review, called AAR. This is a truth-telling session during which everyone has the opportunity to say, "I screwed up," and, "That's something we won't do again." It is also a time to replay key decisions.

Like US Navy SEALs, I'd like my team to have my back, as I have theirs. Here are more questions you can ask:

"Anyone have any great ideas?"
"Tell me what's wrong with this strategy."
"What's really going on around here?"
"What's the best final plan?"

The leader is there to listen, observe, understand, and provide help. Walkabouts are often the best way for leaders to talk with people, both team and patients, listen to everyone, and manage the results. How good is your radar?

TRUST THROUGH UNCERTAINTY

Unless you have courage, a courage that keeps you going,
always going, no matter what happens,
there is no certainty of success.

–Henry Ford

The oath of a team is that we have each other's backs. Your team must understand that you are there for one another. Working together through difficult times builds loyalty and trust. Conquering adversity results in strength, mutual appreciation, and gratitude. In the end, leading through uncertainty forges a stronger, more successful team.

In his book, *The Ideal Team Player*, Patrick Lencioni presents a test which you can take with your team. It will point out individual weaknesses and improvement opportunities for the entire office. It is from this exercise that my team came up with our team virtues:

We are humble.
We are willing to do all work.
We are hungry.
We are each responsible and have a passion for our mission.
We are smart.
We are each aware of our actions and our impact on others.

Even a superstar can be a poor team player or leader. No one wants to work with a self-centered egomaniac. Be humble. When you make a mistake or do something that hurts another person, apologize. Compliment others. It's not all about you. Share the credit. These are the foundations of working together.

Being hungry means displaying a passion for the tasks that needs to be done. Where there is enthusiasm, there is joy, meaning, and fulfillment. Work is love made visible. If you are truly hungry, and want success, your performance will exceed expectations every time.

When we speak about being smart, we are not just talking about having the brain power to do a job correctly. For ideal team dynamics, there are qualities just as important as intellectual capability: emotional intelligence and common sense, which are akin to situational awareness. Emotional intelligence enables you to adjust your behavior to suit any situation. For ideal teamwork and a high-performing team, you want your impact to be favorable at all times.

Listening to and helping others are "smart" behaviors. Being interested in others makes others interested in you. Seeing the best in people is another "smart" trait. Having control of your actions is being smart. These forward-facing attitudes enable a group of individuals to work together. All of these qualities will make you a valuable member of a high-performing team and a good team leader as well.

APPRECIATION

> *Trade your "expectation" for "appreciation"*
> *and your world changes instantly.*
> –Tony Robbins

Keep appreciation in your motivational toolbox. Try this. Give a hand-written, personalized thank-you to each member of your team. Include a $25 gift card. At the bottom of the card, mention one thing that you would like to accomplish in the coming month. State a goal, something like, "I know that we can get to forty-two exams this month," or, "I know we can reach our goal of eighteen to twenty-five new-patient starts," or, "I know that we could get twenty-five new doctors to refer to our office." Then, get out of the way and see what happens. You might just be amazed.

In his book, *The Culture Code*, author Daniel Coyle states that giving attention to people and their actions increases their results threefold. This was studied in the organizational behavior lab at the Massachusetts Institute of Technology (MIT) in a very simple experiment of people making jigsaw puzzles. With one group, nothing was said to the puzzle maker. In the second group, a comment was made about the puzzle maker's progress. This one small act of verbal acknowledgement increased the second puzzle maker's productivity significantly.

It is our job as business leaders to encourage our team's progress. This is not micromanagement. This is showing that you care. You notice the contributions that each team member makes and you acknowledge them. You appreciate them and the work they do, not only for the sake of the business, but also for each other.

A Positive Look at Failure

> *You will never truly know yourself*
> *unless tested by adversity.*
>
> –J. K. Rowlings

We all fail. Some failure in life is inevitable unless you are so cautious that you fail to live life to the fullest, in which case you fail by default. The benefits of failure include the stripping away of the nonessentials and the realization of what truly is. It's what you do after failure that matters. Breakdowns are necessary for breakthroughs.

If you own your dental practice, you are the primary stakeholder in its success. But there are other stakeholders as well, including everyone who works in your organization. Every member of your team is a link in the chain. It is your courageous leadership that includes their career, their hopes, and their dreams.

As the leader of your dental practice, you ultimately decide on priorities. Not everyone on the team may agree. But you will need to work with your stakeholders, your team, to let them candidly know the challenges that you and your organization face. Practice open-book management. Share your numbers. This will help to build consensus through the priorities of a unified team, all rowing in the same direction.

FIVE WAYS TO SAVE TIME

If you want to make good use of your time,
you've got to know what's most important
and then give it all you've got.

–Lee Iacocca

While effective management is putting first things first, effective leadership is deciding what are the first things (strategy). Once you decide upon your first thing (tactics) to accomplish today, reclaim your time to achieve it.

What if you had one extra hour to call new patients? Do you know how powerful that would be? Yet most doctors will say, "I don't have time."

Here are five ways to reclaim your time.

1. PUT DOWN YOUR CELL PHONE.

The time that we spend scrolling through social media and watching videos adds up. Stop social media during working hours unless you are posting to your patients or the public. Text messaging other dentists does little to help you in your practice. Focus on the patients right in front of you. Save the weekend for socializing either in-person or on "social" media.

2. LIMIT CHECKING EMAILS.

The management consulting firm McKinsey reports that professionals spend approximately twenty-eight percent of their work day checking emails. That's about two and a half hours per day! Try to limit checking emails to the start and end of each day, or at lunch. Spend more time with your patients and your team in the running of your practice.

3. BUY TIME.

If there is a time-saving hire, such as a personal assistant to help with society business, go for it. Additional help can make you more productive, keep you organized, and reduce stress, while keeping you focused on your top priorities, your patients, your practice, and your family.

4. *KEEP FOOD HANDY.*

I keep microwaveable soups available for a quick in-office lunch. I often eat at my desk while completing a project. Going out to lunch with a colleague is well worth the time. But otherwise, you might as well stay in your office, eat quickly, and get on with your day.

5. *MAKE THE MOST OF YOUR COMMUTE.*

Call your early morning receptionist and review the day's schedule during your drive to work. Please, do keep your eyes on the road as you use the hands-free speakerphone. This brief pre-huddle can be an invaluable, time-saving start to your day.

Chapter 19

UNITY

All for one, and one for all,
united we stand, divided we fall.
—Alexandre Demas

O n a great team, you won't hear, "I." You'll hear, "We." At some point, the personalities are replaced by a regime of results. You win or lose as a team. The whole is greater than the sum of the parts. You've achieved the synergy of individuals truly working together.

A great team builds confidence in its members. In the dental office, a great team also builds confidence, comfort, and trust with patients. Once you come together as a team, it's easier to build business momentum, month after month, quarter after quarter, year after year.

THREE ACTIONS FOR A UNIFIED TEAM

Clarity of organizational actions will be documented in your Team Handbook, Policies and Procedures, and Organizational Bylaws. These define:

Why do we exist? How do we behave? What do we do? What is most important? Who must do what? How will we succeed?

Three actions for ideal teamwork include:

1. *Creation of organizational clarity.*
2. *Over-communication of organizational order.*
3. *Reinforcement of performance standards of the team.*

Organizational clarity begins with the leader. As CEO, it will be your job to review organizational guidelines, to build a clear vision, and to get things done. It's the small things, done well, which define the success of your practice.

The Most Important Team Member: The Customer

> *Customer service shouldn't just be a department,*
> *it should be the entire company.*
> –Tony Hsieh

Let's not forget our most important team member: our customer. Be sure to ask for feedback at the end of your treatment. On the patient survey should appear the all-important question: "On a scale of 1 to 10, How likely are you to recommend our office to a friend?" If less than a ten, you definitely need to facilitate some valuable feedback.

Include another important query: "Why did you choose our office over others?" From the responses, you will learn the key features of your practice to which your patient connects. These are your core attributes, the heart of your office. With this knowledge, you can make these best aspects shine even brighter. Your patient has made a personal choice to see you. You want their experience to be seamless and to become synonymous with your office brand.

In his book, *The Frontline CEO*, Eric Strafel states that Amazon CEO Jeff Bezos includes an empty chair in each meeting to represent the customer. This serves as a constant reminder that the customer is everyone's boss. Another exercise is to begin and end each team meeting with a quote or review from a customer. The more that you listen to the real experiences of your customers, the easier it will be to deliver service with the customer in mind. Remember to solicit constructive criticism and negative comments, too. Not only do you need to emphasize the positive,

but a great leader wants to know about problem areas in order to eliminate the negative.

THE MOST IMPORTANT PLACE: YOUR LOCAL COMMUNITY

Where your patients live, your immediate practice area, deserves attention. Chances are that your community is pretty tight-knit. Your families
know each other, and word-of-mouth from patients is most likely your
top referral source. Get involved with community projects and bring your
office into your local city and suburbs.

As I write this book, we are holding a Thanksgiving food drive for the
Contra Costa County foodbank. This announcement goes out to every
patient in our database, to all of our referring doctors, and to our entire
community. In this way, we are civic leaders. Take time to promote the
common good.

Dentists are also a great educational resource. Support schools by
being a speaker or career mentor. Kids love to hear how their biology
class applies to becoming a dentist. Even the teachers enjoy hearing about
deciduous and succedaneous teeth. Give out some fun holiday themed
toothbrushes with your office logo to the students at the same visit to
make it memorable.

Relationships with other dentists create the foundation for excellent
interdisciplinary treatment for your patients. Participation in your local
dental societies and study clubs fuels networking excellence. Study clubs
such as the Spear Study Club and the Seattle Club make continued learning together fun.

ORGANIZATIONAL ORDER

> *If an organization is tolerant of everything,*
> *it will stand for nothing.*
> –Patrick Lencioni

There will be times when your team rejects employment law, or your
society ignores Policies and Procedures or Bylaws. As the leader, you

must hold fast and not allow this to happen. When situations are undesirable or even unprofessional, you must keep communication open with and continue to work for the people you serve: your patients, families, colleagues, and profession. Always strive to maintain organizational order in your office and voluntary societies. Be prepared and stay strong.

You may face similar humiliating acts when the dental politicians who grab for power in your dental organization under your leadership grab for attention. Be prepared and stay strong. Childlike behavior is humiliating to them, and shocking to others. When confronted with "snarky" or cynical behavior, always maintain your dignity, upholding the values and vision of your group. Be a force for good.

SIXTEEN ACTIONS OF A PROFESSIONAL

The goal of our professional behavior is to best serve the patient, our community, and each other. Here are sixteen signs of professionalism. Take some time to discuss and review these actions of a professional with your team.

1. *Put the customer first.*
2. *Listen to the needs of the customer.*
3. *Learn to understand the customer.*
4. *Look for ways to improve the customer experience.*
5. *Anticipate what needs to be done.*
6. *Seek responsibility.*
7. *Take pride in your work.*
8. *Do whatever is necessary to get the job done.*
9. *Be fully engaged.*
10. *Be eager to learn.*
11. *Work to improve.*
12. *Be trustworthy.*
13. *Be honest and loyal.*
14. *Be a team player.*
15. *Speak respectfully.*
16. *Look clean, neat, and well-dressed.*

THREE TRAITS OF A MERITOCRACY

Psychological safety allows for moderate risk-taking,
speaking your mind, creativity, and sticking your neck out
without fear of having it cut off.
–Laura Delizonna

It will be your biggest leadership challenge to build, maintain, and motivate your desired performance standards through respectful communication. When giving and receiving feedback, stay aware that human beings are complex. Your employees and colleagues will never shoot the messenger if you remember that people are sensitive.

In his book, *Principles: Life and Work,* Ray Dalio writes that the success of his company depends upon achieving a real meritocracy, which he states has three characteristics:

1. **Putting honest thoughts out on the table;**
2. **Having thoughtful disagreements where people are willing to be open-minded and learn; and**
3. **Having agreed-upon ways of moving beyond disagreements without resentments.**

He calls this environment the "radical candor" of truthful transparency. In this environment, you need to allow people to see and say almost anything.

Try this exercise. Have everyone on your team write down how they rate the open communication level of your team meetings on a scale of zero to five. Collect the ballots and take the average. If you score a three or below, something is not being addressed. What is it?

The key obstacle to candor is lack of psychological safety. Team members must feel secure in their positions in order to risk speaking out openly. Professor Amy C. Edmondson of the Harvard Business School notes that people who feel psychologically safe tend to be more innovative, learn from mistakes, and are motivated to improve their team and company. Studies at Google show that feeling secure enough to speak out is one factor that all high-performing teams exhibit. Built on the backbone of serving, sharing, and caring, candor and psychological safety maintain maximal team functioning.

MUTUAL TRUST

When there is trust,
conflict becomes nothing but the pursuit of truth,
an attempt to find the best possible answer.
–Patrick Lencioni

Mutual trust is the confidence that intentions are good and ethical. There is nothing to hide. There is no reason to be protective around anyone in the group. Everyone is relaxed and free to be themselves.

Disingenuous behavior or political pursuits destroy trust. Competition among the team and professional colleagues needs to be turned off, and the instincts of what is good for everyone in the group need to be turned on in order to build mutual trust.

To foster trust, the leader must also reward vulnerability. Although I have never fired anyone in thirty-two years of owning my practice, many times a team member has said to me, "Are you going to fire me?" during a difficult conversation. My response is, **"I trust that we will work this out."** Losing one's job is an underlying fear. To battle this fear and to build confidence, it is important to assure all team members that you want "only the truth to be spoken. Whether good or bad, you need to know the truth," without reproach. Team members need confidence in the leader and in themselves to always remain truthful.

What happens when you have a non-vulnerable, non-trusting (and non-trusted) team member? This person is hiding something that can't be faced. There is a heavy burden. This person will eventually quit.

RESPECT

> *Our strength as a nation comes in our unity.*
> *We are the United States of America,*
> *not the divided states.*
> —Ben Carson

When I think of respect, I envision listening to each person's perspective. Everyone deserves to be valued, especially those who serve. Respect can be delivered by how we speak to each other. Saying please and thank you. Using the term "Doctor." Giving full attention without distraction. Not interrupting.

Respect can be given to work also. Paying attention to details and being organized is giving your work respect. How your staff dress and act gives respect to themselves and others. Behavior is a sign of respect for everyone in the surrounding environment.

TEAM COHESION

> *There is more power in unity than division.*
> —Emanuel Cleaver

A unified team makes every day a delight. There are no interpersonal squabbles and communication is positive. Teamwork is easy when everyone gets along.

I remember my first realization that I had a team problem. If you notice lack of camaraderie, start with the first teamwork exercise: sharing of vulnerability and building of trust.

At your next team meeting, ask some simple descriptions: tell us about your siblings, describe your unique challenges of childhood, tell us about your first job, describe your worst job, then listen.

Simply by describing these challenges, team members start to see one another as human beings. Empathy develops. Staff can begin to treat each other with fairness as their mutual understanding improves. Doing this exercise contributes to breaking down barriers and working toward team cohesion.

Music, The Ideal Example of Leadership and Teamwork

Problems arise in the dental office or organization when all do not appreciate that leadership is responsible for knowing all systems. Team members who consider leadership as "micromanagement" destroy the organizational system and produce chaos. With these misperceptions, things run amok and anarchy results.

A symphony orchestra is perhaps the ideal example of leadership and teamwork. The conductor needs to know each player's part. He doesn't "delegate" the responsibility of knowing the parts. He doesn't play the part. The conductor as leader brings all parts together, understanding how each part fits into the musical performance.

In a symphony orchestra, everyone must play at the same speed or tempo led by the conductor. Everyone follows the conductor, and following the leader is not voluntary. It is a necessity. Otherwise, the ensemble can't play together.

The team of orchestra players and conductor must be in total alignment. Communication is visual, auditory, and physical. Musicians read the conductor's body language to work together. Leadership and teamwork come together, and everyone plays in perfect harmony. At the end, the conductor acknowledges the team, and everyone shares in a celebration of success. How wonderful it would be if our offices and dental organizations could work on a high organizational level similar to a symphony orchestra.

Chapter 20

SUCCESS

When you are surrounded by people
who share a passionate commitment around a common purpose,
anything is possible.

–Howard Schultz

I t is the relationships, integrity, and love which I remember most favorably in my journey of service, teamwork, and leadership. It is what we were able to accomplish together, with our patients, in our community, with our referring dentists, and with each other that gives our lives meaning and significance.

When you feel that you have reached a milestone of success, take time to celebrate. Recognize the team. Acknowledge the contributions of each individual. Encourage team members to do the same. Everyone benefits from a "job well done" shout-out.

The publication *Investor's Business Daily* has spent years analyzing successful leaders and teams. What they have found is ten common traits that, when combined, can turn dreams into reality.

TEN TRAITS FOR BUSINESS SUCCESS

1. GOAL-ORIENTED

It is the last hour of the month in the dental office. Did you reach your goal? When you are keeping score, you work with intensity. You are inspired. You tell yourself, "We can do it!" Work becomes a game of fourth-quarter football. Everyone is cheering, "Let's get across the finish line." Know the score at all times. Seeing a new patient or starting a new-patient procedure is like "scoring a basket" or "getting the ball in the end zone" for the team.

Setting goals applies not only to professional life but also to personal life. Each year on New Year's Eve, my family and I write down our top-ten favorite moments of the past year as well as our top-ten goals for the new year. This simple activity focuses our energies. It's fun to look back at the previous goals through the years. We keep our notes in a little leather notebook, and are gratified when many of our goals actively become a reality. One of my personal top-ten goals was to publish this book!

2. TAKE ACTION

> *Thinking doesn't achieve outcomes, only action does.*
> –Tim S. Grover

Good things come to those who take action. Ask yourself, "What is the one thing that I could do right now to achieve my most important goal?" Go for it!

Without action, goals are just dreams. Taking action in your dental practice—especially in the treatment coordination process—is so important I wrote a whole book about it! *Take Action: Treatment Coordination for a Successful Dental Practice* set my practice in a more profitable and efficient direction. I can say that, having implemented the action items detailed in that book, I have never enjoyed practice success more.

Tackle each action item one at a time and see it through to completion. Pick one thing to accomplish each day. Finish it. In a year, you will have completed 365 actions that will guarantee your success.

3. KEEP LEARNING

When you are a CEO, leader, or president of your organization, from where are you going to get great ideas, inspiration, and advice? I've heard that most Fortune 500 CEOs read on average one business book every week. Look toward those who can help you. Journals, books, podcasts, mentors, and coaches are great places to start for lifelong learning.

4. ANALYZE DETAILS

The key to puzzle-making is finding the smallest detail in each piece which leads to a fit. The more you look, the more you see. Suddenly, the big picture of the fit becomes clear. It's the same in business. Take time to see all the small but vitally important details of a situation and gather all the facts. Hear both sides. Get as much feedback as you can. Learn from your mistakes, which once revealed can teach you the most important lessons and set you on a clear path to success.

Dig into your office management systems. Look at every report, contract, payment, and deposit. Make a habit of monitoring snail mail. Dental practice management is like one giant puzzle with many moving pieces. When all the pieces fit perfectly, you can feel the satisfaction and confidence in what you have achieved.

5. FOCUS TIME AND MONEY

It is hard to live without money. In fact, I would say it is impossible for a healthy lifestyle to be out of cash. Be careful with your money, both in the office and in your personal life. Wise money management will help you to lead a peaceful, low-stress life. This can be achieved.

Manage your time as you manage your business and money. There are only so many hours in the day and in your life. Use them wisely. Don't let other people waste your valuable time. Schedule your own "hour of power." Close the office door, leave others behind, and get done what you need to get done for success. Of course, make family time a top priority.

6. BE COMFORTABLE BEING DIFFERENT

> *Define success on your own terms,*
> *achieve it by your own rules,*
> *and build a life you're proud to live.*
> —Anne Sweeney

The thought, "What will people think?" need never enter your mind. Who cares? Following the herd is a sure way to mediocrity. Don't waste time on group think. Be bold, creative, and innovative. Focus on *your* individual goals and priorities.

7. COMMUNICATE EFFECTIVELY

> *You can have the greatest idea in the world,*
> *but if you can't communicate your ideas,*
> *it doesn't matter.*
> —Steve Jobs

In a leadership forum, former PepsiCo CEO Indra Nooyi described how she met with Steve Jobs and asked him what she could do to improve her leadership skills. Jobs told her, "Sometimes you need to use powerful and effective language. Swear a little!" Nooyi says that this was not in her nature, but she tried it. It was highly effective!

Male leaders might get angry when they communicate. They might use evocative language to create a sense of urgency. Driven by passion, women can get emotional during difficult situations. Use your verbal skills to motivate, whether you are a man or a woman.

In their book, *Work with Me,* authors Barbara Annis and John Gray outline the eight blind spots and differences between men and women working together. One blind spot is that women express their emotions when they communicate. Men, in general, do not. Women focus on collaboration. Men focus on hierarchy.

In her book, *When Women Lead,* author Julia Boostin describes collective intelligence studies of working groups and the benefit of an "outsider," a new participant, to increased team performance. She notes that fresh perspectives produced "social sensitivity," motiving all group members to work harder, explain their thinking more, and review data more carefully to arrive at solutions with more accuracy. These studies revealed that conversational turn taking was the hallmark of the most innovative groups and that women are more conscientious about asking everyone in the group for their opinion and participation. Women in a group increased innovation. In studies done at Northwestern University Business School, teams with more women scored higher in innovation. To be clear: teams didn't perform better if they had a woman, or an equal number of men and women, they performed better if they had *more* women.

Whether you are a man or a woman, it takes courage to call out and eliminate bad group behaviors. If you find yourself in this uncomfortable leadership situation, whether in the office or on your dental board, continue to interact respectfully but with candor and vigor, letting the troublesome person know, "You have a choice; we will win with or without you."

Deliver the message. To be a leader, one must sometimes be explicitly candid in order to achieve success.

8. TAKE RESPONSIBILITY

I own this.

–Tim S. Grover

Legendary personal coach Tim S. Grover describes in his book, *Relentless: From Good to Great to Unstoppable,* the drive embodied in a person whom he calls "A Cleaner," one who doesn't have to love the hard work, but craves the end results. This person has complete focus, they're in "the zone," and they never let up. This team member overcomes whatever obstacle stands in their way. They take responsibility. Failure is not an option. They're the first to say, "I've got this."

As leader, you must take ownership for everyone in your organization, the good and the bad. You are responsible for the performance of your team. You do everything that you can to influence motivation and behavior, performance, results, and excellence. Repeat this leadership mantra: "If it is to be, it's up to me."

I hold my team to a high standard. It's my name on my office door and my reputation that is on the line for work that we do together. It's their name and photo on the wall, together with our mission: "*Caring professionals serving valued patients.*"

There are no bonuses in life for "trying hard." Results-based rewards send the message that the score matters.

9. Positivity

> *If you want to reach for success in every area of your life,*
> *the most important asset you can have*
> *is a faithfully optimistic winning attitude.*
> –Dr. Nido R. Qubein

If you are an optimist, always thinking, expecting, and working toward success, then your mindset will carry you through the difficult times which every person and company will eventually experience.

One negative attitude can change the entire dynamic of a winning team. A clinically depressed person is not a good fit for the customer service of a dental office. A bully is not an ideal team member for a non-profit volunteer board of directors of a dental society. Success lies in surrounding yourself with people who are persistently positive, despite the vicissitudes of the work environment.

10. Perseverance

> *Patience, persistence, and perspiration*
> *make an unbeatable combination for success.*
> –Napoleon Hill

As Chief Executive Officer (from the verb, to execute, meaning "to put into effect"), I sometimes need to handle difficult situations in order to accomplish the necessary tasks. My job is a responsibility. And, I love it! Leaders never give up when confronted with obstacles. They persevere until they come up with a solution. Some may even call this trait "stubbornness." It is also the realization and understanding that you, as leader, have the most thankless role in the company. Leaders do their job with pride, often alone, and without complaint. Because as a leader, you are a servant, and that is what you signed up for.

Focus and grit are the fuel of achievement. Never give up. Success is a marathon. Persistence in all things cannot be overestimated. Work a little every day toward your goals. They will be achieved. Be thankful that you can make a difference in this world through your work. Work is love made visible. That's why we chose to lead in the first place.

STRENGTHEN BUSINESS RELATIONSHIPS

One year after our annual advance, I asked my team to pick their one word for the coming year. My team suggested, "love, growth, thankful, balance, and care." I responded with the word, "engage." As a team, we agreed that for one year we would live our word.

After the long pandemic lockdown in California, I felt that we needed to redouble our engagement efforts. I mailed, called, visited, and lunched with my dental colleagues. I rejoined my local Seattle Study Club, and I helped start a new Spear Study Club in our community. I'm happy to report that I have achieved eighteen new relationships through the word "engage." It has been a rewarding project. Dare I say it was catalytic and life-changing?

Left unattended, your business relationships will cool. It is your job to stoke those embers. In my book, *It All Starts with Marketing: 201 Marketing Tips for Growing a Dental Practice,* I describe that a lunch meeting is not only about engagement and friendship but also a business meeting. You are mixing business with pleasure.

Start your week by making ten phone calls to people with whom you want to do business. Put together your dental office referral list and leave it on your desk. It will need to be constantly updated as new dental colleagues join your community and others move away or retire.

Another "engagement" opportunity is to drop by dental offices to say hello. Think of how you feel when your dental rep drops in to do so. It brightens your day. Do you buy something from your rep? Of course, you do! The same is true for you with your colleagues. Take time to grow your business through emphasizing personal relationships.

ELIMINATE THE CLUTTER

> *Order is intelligence.*
> –Johann Wolfgang von Goethe

Entropy is a measure of the degree of randomness and disorder of a system. For an isolated system, entropy is high due to high disorder. As uniformity of the structure decreases, entropy increases. Heat increases entropy.

For your dental office or volunteer society, entropy is not good. In your office, cleanliness reflects clinical excellence to your patients. You want your office to be spotless. Look at everything that your patient looks at, floor to ceiling. Fix what can be improved.

Disorder happens in your dental practice management systems. If left unchecked, your financial reports will start to become less attended. Apathy will set in. As the leader, you will find yourself in a state of continuously cleaning-up reports.

This happens in dental societies as well. Systems are not checked. Rules are not followed. Without leadership, organizational behavior falls into chaos. The meeting is not called. Bylaws and Policies and Procedures are not followed. All of these systems need attention to ensure proper actions, compliance, and necessary updates.

I have a joyful habit: the day before I leave on vacation, I clean my desk. There is satisfaction in knowing that your work is done, your desk is cleared, and it's time to relax. The amazing thing is, no matter how many times I clean my desk, before the next vacation, it will need to be cleaned again.

Purge your unnecessary clutter. Once eliminated, it is easier to focus on what is important. Go through everything: your storage unit, closets, drawers, desk top, and bookcases. Take time to have an office clean-up day. Let your office shine. You will feel great in the process.

Team or Family?

*Don't just hire people to fit the first job they will do;
hire people you want to share your life with.*
                                        –Ray Dalio

My business is a "family business." It is owned and operated by me and my family. That being said, the team that works in my office knows my family, interacts with my family, and in one respect, is an extension of my family. Family thinking spills over into my office. Whatever advice I would give my child, I give my team. The atmosphere is trusting.

Individuals are responsible for their own tasks without language or protocol getting in the way. People know what lane they are swimming in, and they know how the team interacts as a whole. We have team lunches and outings. We celebrate birthdays and special occasions such as weddings, retirements, or baby showers.

We all spend too much time at work to be uncomfortable. Your team members should be treated like guests in your home. You invited them. When people feel that they are at home, where they belong, then great attitudes, high morale, and productivity will follow.

Your Best

*All I ask is that today,
you do the best work of your entire life.*
                                        –Steve Jobs

Best is personal dedication. Best is a way of life. It starts with the best thinking and the best attitude that results in the best work, for the best life.

I hope that this book will produce your best leadership and collaboration for your best team. Just by reading this book, you have raised your game of dental practice management. As you near the conclusion of this book, take a moment to thank your team and give out a few achievement awards for what you have accomplished together. Examples could include:

Best Attitude
High Scorer
Most Improved
Most Inspirational
Best Team Player

Truly felt accolades are not to be taken lightly. The awards are not tokens or corny. The winners have earned this distinction. All of their hard work is recognized and appreciated. As each person accepts their award, you will see a beaming face and a sense of pride.

Such moments are priceless and help foster the motivation needed to continue to achieve. So, ring the bell! Give praise. Give applause. Give the bonus. Have a special celebration for each win.

I end this book with what may be called the lost secret of leadership: encouragement, which is the key to high self-esteem, higher productivity, and the highest achievement. Your encouragement may be the very action that propels someone over the finish line.

Fun

*The missing element in most professionals'
lives is the most important.
They often already have money, prestige, title, and standing.
What they don't have is fun.*
–David H. Maister

"I love this!" I hope that this is what you will say when you do the work which makes you successful. Fun is the ultimate reward.

There is lots to love in dentistry, from freedom and equity, to being your own boss, to working with a great team, to serving loveable patients. There is joy in making people happy, relieving their dental pain, and helping them to look and feel beautiful.

Running a business well is fun. I hope that after reading this book, you will be able to keep the engine of your practice machine running smoothly, and that it will become less stressful and more enjoyable.

Enthusiasm, knowledge, organization, courage, persistence, grit, gratefulness, energy, and love will help you achieve a successful and happy life. Those who ultimately achieve major success manage to capture the magic of minor achievements each day. Your daily habits ensure your success.

A New Look at Teamwork

Ancora Imparo.
I am still learning.
—Michelangelo, age 87

A leader does not build a business. A leader assembles a team which builds a business. You can seize the opportunities of working together if you stay humble. Each day we benefit from one another. We learn from our teams, our patients, and our colleagues. We grow by reading books and by pursuing excellence. The more that you learn about leadership and teamwork, the more you will love it. Eventually, it will become a game, not a struggle. That is your goal, to love what you do. Once we can all do that, we can share what we love with each other. That is the greatest gift of all.

A New Look at Leadership

The fundamental role of a leader
is to look for ways to shape the decades ahead,
not just react to the present,
and to help others accept the discomfort of
disruptions to the status quo.
—Indra Nooyi

There is only one type of leadership: servant leadership. Your ultimate success is to fulfill your personal calling. With perseverance, your business plan will ultimately succeed. It will not, however, be without challenges that you will need to overcome. You will need to learn to be a better leader, a better team member, and a stronger and wiser person.

Perhaps after reading this book, you will take a new look at yourself, your leadership, and your team, evaluating situations with a new understanding. I know that I have. There is no finish line to your professional development.

Perhaps you will change your perspective on strategy *with* your team rather than strategy *for* your team. Perhaps you will orient your thinking toward developing a team of leaders as the best way to grow your organization. Your team members are the coauthors of your shared success. Your meetings and communication skills may have a renewed focus on results. You may realize for the first time that your success lies in working with, and your ability to lead, your team. Dentistry, leadership, and teamwork are noble pursuits. I hope that this book has given you new insights. Here's to your success!

CONCLUSION

Be the change you wish to see in the world.
*   –Mahatma Gandhi*

The goal of being of service to others is an inexhaustible source of inspiration. I hope this book about leadership and teamwork will help improve your leadership skills and create a high-performing team. Your increased awareness of leadership obligations and teamwork coaching will help you to conquer future challenges that you may face in your dental office. I fervently believe that the skills acquired and implemented from this book can transform your organization, make you more fulfilled and successful, and eliminate business management suffering.

What you do now is a new beginning. How you approach your day, after learning new leadership and teamwork skills, can have a wonderful effect not just on your day, but on your entire life.

You are not alone in your daily challenges of dental practice management and leadership. I hope that having read this book will contribute to your professional joy, happiness, and effectiveness as a team player or leader of your team.

Teamwork is about people and it requires a leader. That leader is you. Take charge, take center stage, and take action, with your team, and with yourself.

We can do no great things, only small things with great love.
*   –Mother Teresa*

Teamwork can be the most rewarding aspect of your daily office life. There is nothing better than working with a gelled team. You will spend more time with your dental team than you might with your own spouse, so gather and surround yourself with your team members wisely.

We're all in it together, this wonderful thing called dentistry. At your dental office, you're a team. On your dental society board, you're a team. Together, make every day the best that it can be and accomplish something great. Enjoy every moment and each other. At the end of it all, leave with grace and celebrate. And, remember, it's one team, one score. Through leadership, teamwork, and collaboration, you can make the changes you wish to see in the world.

I leave you with one final story and thoughts on the importance of words in leadership and teamwork. In recent years, my husband learned that he loves to cook. We call him "The Surgical Chef." Growing up, he didn't have much opportunity to learn culinary skills because he was surrounded by strong women who showed tremendous leadership and teamwork skills in the kitchen.

One day, after his mother died, he came across a spiral-bound notebook containing treasured, handwritten family recipes collected by his great-aunt Agnes. Like my own grandparents who immigrated to the US from Poland before World War I, she worked in a textile mill as a seamstress. She also worked as a part-time waitress.

On the cover of Aunt Agnes' treasured cookbook was taped the following summary, entitled, "A Short Course in Human Relations." I call it a short course in leadership, teamwork, and collaboration. Here are the important words:

6 words:
I ADMIT I MADE A MISTAKE
5 words:
YOU DID A GREAT JOB
4 words:
WHAT IS YOUR OPINION
3 words:
IF YOU PLEASE
2 words:

THANK YOU
1 word:
WE

This spiral notebook is now Aunt Agnes' legacy, which lives on in my husband and in our family. Whether you realize it or not, your dental practice or your dental society is part of your legacy. It matters not just to you, but also to all who love you, and to all whom you love and serve. Great people leave legacies and you have the chance to create your own legacy.

Leaders work hard until the last minute of their last day. Be one of those people. Leave your own legacy. Begin and end your leadership and teamwork journey with the word "We."

ACKNOWLEDGEMENTS

It's a luxury being a writer,
because all you ever think about is life.

–Amy Tan

M y leadership and teamwork journey has been a long one. Never could I have imagined all that I would learn from the time I graduated from dental school to where I am today, more than thirty years later. The experience has been educational and rewarding.

I am extremely grateful to all the people who have helped me along the way and to those who inspired me during the writing of this book.

Thank you first and foremost to my own team at Gorczyca Orthodontics: Lyndsay, Jessica, Madison, Leona, and Jolene. You are an amazing team and I am proud of what we can achieve together. I am grateful each day to work with you and proud to be your leader.

Thank you to the Northern California Angle Society of Orthodontists for all that you have taught me through my years of service, teamwork, and leadership. Thank you to my sponsor, Dr. Bob Boyd for believing in me. Thank you to Dr. Gary Baughman and Carol Baughman for your education on Parliamentary Procedure. Thank you for the leadership coaching, mentorship, and encouragement. Thank you to Dr. Ken Kai for being the first to invite me to the board. Thank you to Dr. Ron and Karen Champion for their tireless dedication to Bylaws reform and service to the society. Thank you to Dr. Jae Park for his exemplary representation of our society's core values of clinical excellence, scientific inquiry, service to the profession, and fellowship.

Thank you to Jon Gordon for his books and optimism, which continue to inspire leaders, teams, and coaches worldwide. Thank you for your generosity in writing an endorsement for this book.

Thank you to my leadership coach Amy Hiett of the Table Group. It has been an honor to work with you. Your executive coaching and experience with leaders and leadership was invaluable to me as a woman leader. Thank you for your wisdom and advice during this leadership and writing journey.

A big, tall thank you to Bernie Stoltz for his coaching, optimism, and "Bernisms," which energize coaches and dentists nationwide. Knowing you is a win-win. I am proud to call you my friend. Thank you for writing the Foreword to this book.

Thank you to Aimee Nevins of Fortune Management for her valuable teamwork and leadership coaching through the years, especially in the area of communication. Thank you for your support and friendship.

Thank you to Dino Watts for your advice in the writing of this book and for your emphasis on story telling. Your insights on leadership make the responsibilities of practice ownership clearer and your teamwork presentations make being part of a dental team and dental meeting fun.

Thank you to professional and long-time friend Sahar Jaffrey, Pediatric Dentist, for your leadership and service to the dental profession. I will never forget filming the podcast "#569 Six Specialists" for Dentistry Uncensored with Howard Farran. https://ww.youtube.com/watch?v=vKEKvf9PTJ8. What a great day that was for women specialists in the dental profession.

Thank you to Michelle Shimmin for your support, friendship, and contributions to the orthodontic profession.

Thank you to Angus Pryor for your dedication, encouragement, dental practice management knowledge, and kind review of this book all the way from Australia!

A big thank you to attorney Phil Finn for reading and editing Chapter 3 and for his wisdom and advise on Employment Law.

To Phil Vogels, Neal Kravitz, and everyone at *The Journal of Clinical Orthodontics:* Thank you for including me on your team. It is an honor for me to work with all of you. Thank you for your valuable contributions to the orthodontic profession.

Thank you to my publisher, Stephanie Chandler of Authority Publishing, for your commitment to excellence in publishing and for your work on this, our fifth book together. Thank you for helping me make my writing goals a reality.

To my family team, my husband, Richard J., and my son, Richard F.: I'm happy to be a member of your team. I respect the capable leadership of my husband, of whom I've always said, if he were not an orthopedic surgeon, he would make an excellent military general. Thank you for your organizational skills, ethics, love, and editing of this manuscript. Thank you to my son for his excellent behavior and achievements. You make us proud to be part of your team and I hope and pray that someday you will become a contributing leader in society.

Thank you most of all to my readers, who encourage me, inspire me, and who have read this book to the end. You make my writing adventure exciting and worthwhile. I wish you much success. You have taught me most of all that one does not need a title to be a leader. I love being part of your team. Thank you from the bottom of my heart.

Appendix 1

LEADERSHIP AND TEAMWORK BLANK TEMPLATE

	Leader	**Team**	**Together**
Jan			
Feb			
Mar			
Apr			
May			
June			
July			
Aug			
Sept			
Oct			
Nov			
Dec			

Appendix 2

LEADERSHIP AND TEAMWORK SAMPLE TEMPLATE

Month	Leader	Team	Together
Jan	Annual Team Advance 4 Advance Questions	Achievement Awards	Annual Advance New Team Photo
Feb	Personal Office Clean-Up Day	Cross-Training	DISC Profile Musical Instrument Question
Mar	Conduct Annual HR Reviews	Attitude Test	First Quarter Team Building Outing
Apr	Review Core Values	Review Benefits of Excellence	Team Appreciation Survey
May	Clean Desk and Drawers	The Immersion Exercise	What We See: Young/Old Woman Exercise
June	Rate Open Communication	The 5 Dysfunctions Test	Second Quarter Team Building Outing
July	10 Questions	"We Are" "We Are Not" Culture Exercise	Candor Test
Aug	Assess Interview Candidate Test	Review TO CARE	The Truck Test
Sept	Review The Core Values	Live Your Word Exercise	Third Quarter Team Building Outing
Oct	Review The Vision	Customer Chair Exercise	Growth/Mindset Question
Nov	Review The Mission	Review Customer Quotes from Reviews	What Excites You Question
Dec	Summarize 10 Best Events, 10 Goals for the New Year	End-of-Year Bonus	End-of-Year Celebration

BIBLIOGRAPHY

"About time." *Breathe (2021)*. Lewes, United Kingdom: GMC Publications.

Abrashoff, Captain D. Michael. *It's Our Ship: The No-Nonsense Guide to Leadership.* New York: Business Plus, 2008.

Abrashoff, Captain D. Michael. *It's Your Ship: Management Techniques from the Best Damn Ship in the Navy.* New York: Business Plus, 2002.

American Institute of Parliamentarians Standard Code of Parliamentary Procedure. New York: The McGraw-Hill Companies, 2012.

Annis, Barbara, Gray, John. *Work with Me: The 8 Blind Spots Between Men and Women in Business.* New York: St. Martin's Griffen, 2013.

Barsh, Joanna, and Susie Cranston, and Geoffrey Lewis. *How Remarkable Women Lead: The Breakthrough Model for Work and Life.* New York: Crown Publishing Group, 2011.

Boorstin, Julia. *When Women Lead.* New York: Avid Reader Press, 2022.

Brounstein, Marty. *Managing Teams for Dummies.* New York: Wiley Publishing, 2002.

Burns, Ursula M. *Where You Are is not Who You Are.* New York: HarperCollins Publishers, 2021.

Chapman, Gary and Paul White. *The 5 Languages of Appreciation in the Workplace: Empowering Organizations by Encouraging People.* Chicago: Northfield Publishing, 2019.

Cooper, Cary L., PhD, Lynn Holdsworth, PhD, and Sheena Johnson, PhD. *Organizational Behavior for Dummies.* Chichester, West Sussex, England: John Wiley and Sons, 2012.

Covey, Stephen R. *The 7 Habits of Highly Effective People.* New York: Simon & Schuster, Inc. 2004.

Coyle, Daniel. *The Culture Code: The Secrets of Highly Successful Groups.* New York: Bantam Books, 2018.

Csikszentmihalyi, Mihaly. *Good Business: Leadership, Flow, and the Making of Meaning.* New York: Penguin Group, 2004.

Dewar, Carolyn; Keller, Scott; and Malhorta, Vikram. *CEO Excellence.* New York: Simon + Schuster, 2022.

Dixon, Brian and Ruth Soukup. *Start with your People: The Daily Decision That Changes Everything.* Grand Rapids, MI: Zondervan, 2019.

Evans, Henry J. and Elaine Biech. *131 Ways to Win with Accountability: Best Practices for Driving Better Results.* Dallas: CornerStone Leadership Institute, 2018.

Fried, Jason. "Why Work Does Not Happen At Work." *TEDx Talks (August 29, 2012),* https://www.youtube.com/watch?v=0UmUgaJwEr0.

Garry, Joan. *Nonprofit Leadership.* Hoboken, NJ: John Wiley and Sons, Inc., 2017.

George, Bill, and Clayton, Zach. *True North Emerging Leader.* John Wiley & Sons, Inc., Hoboken, New Jersey. 2022.

Gielan, Michelle. *Broadcasting Happiness.* Dallas, Texas: BenBella Books, Inc. 2015.

Gielan, Michelle. "The Power of Positive Communication. *"World Happiness Summit, Miam., (2017)* https://www.youtube.com/watch?v=nlW4nx78SEw

Gitomer, Jeffrey. *Little Book of Leadership: The 12.5 Strengths of Responsible, Reliable, Remarkable Leaders That Create Results, Rewards, and Resilience.* Hoboken, NJ: John Wiley and Sons, Inc., 2011.

Gitomer, Jeffrey. *Little Gold Book of YES! Attitude: How to Find, Build and Keep a YES! Attitude for a Lifetime of Success and Happiness.* FT Press, 2007.

"Global Glee." *Breathe* (2021). Lewes, United Kingdom: GMC Publications.

Gorczyca, Ann Marie. *At Your Service: 5-Star Customer Care for a Successful Dental Practice.* Gold River, CA: Authority Publishing, 2017.

Gorczyca, Ann Marie. *Beyond the Morning Huddle: HR Management for a Successful Dental Practice.* Gold River, CA: Authority Publishing, 2015.

Gorczyca, Ann Marie. *It All Starts with Marketing: 201 Marketing Tips for Growing a Dental Practice.* Gold River, CA: Authority Publishing, 2013.

Gorczyca, Ann Marie. *Take Action: Treatment Coordination for a Successful Dental Practice.* Gold River, CA: Authority Publishing, 2020.

Gordon, Jon. *The Energy Bus.* Hoboken, NJ: John Wiley and Sons, 2007

Gordon, Jon. *The Power of a Positive Team: Proven Principles and Practices that Make Great Teams Great.* Hoboken, NJ: John Wiley and Sons, 2018.

Hackman, J. Richard. *Groups That Work (and Those That Don't).* San Francisco: Jossey-Bass Publishers, 1990.

Hackman, J. Richard. *Leading Teams: Setting the Stage for Great Performances.* Boston: Harvard Business School Press, 2002.

Harvard Business Review, Peter F. Drucker, Daniel Goleman, and Bill George. *HBR's 10 Must Reads On Leadership.* Boston: Harvard Business School Publishing Corporation, 2011.

Hawk, Ryan. *The Pursuit of Excellence.* New York: McGraw Hill, 2022.

Hays, Nick. *Elite: High Performance Lessons and Habits from a Former Navy SEAL.* Hoboken, New Jersey: John Wiley and Sons, Inc, 2019.

Heifetz, Ronald A., Linsky, Marty. *Leadership on the Line.* Boston: Harvard Business Review Press, 2002.

Hoffman, Bryce G. *American Icon: Alan Mulally and the Fight to Save Ford Motor Company.* New York: Crown Publishing Group, 2012.

https://www.dir.ca.gov/databases/oprl/disr-awe.html

https://www.dir.ca.gov/dise/fag_overtime.htm#~:text=Yes%2C%20 if%20it%20is%2 0a,bonuses%20include%20flat%20sum%20bonuses

https://www.dol.gov/agencies/whd/state/meal-breaks

https://health.clevelandclinic.org/what-are-microaggressions-and-examples/

http://www.psychologytoday.com/us/basics/microaggression

Joy, Hubert. *The Heart of Business: Leadership Principles for the Next Era of Capitalism.* Boston: Harvard Business Review Press, 2021.

Julien, Larry. *God is My CEO: Following God's Principles in a Bottom-Line World.* Avon, MA: Adams Media Corporation, 2002.

Krzyzewski, Mike and Jamie K. Spatola. *Beyond Basketball: Coach K's Keywords for Success.* New York: Hachette Book Group, 2006.

Lencioni, Patrick. *Death by Meeting: A Leadership Fable . . . About Solving the Most Painful Problem in Business.* San Francisco: Jossey-Bass, 2004.

Lencioni, Patrick. *Getting Naked: A Business Fable About Shedding The Three Fears That Sabotage Client Loyalty.* San Francisco: Jossey-Bass, 2010.

Lencioni, Patrick M. *The Advantage: Why Organizational Health Trumps Everything Else in Business.* San Francisco: Jossey-Bass, 2012.

Lencioni, Patrick. *The Five Dysfunctions of a Team: A Leadership Fable.* San Francisco: Jossey-Bass, 2002.

Lencioni, Patrick M. *The Ideal Team Player: How to Recognize and Cultivate The Three Essential Virtues.* Hoboken, NJ: John Wiley and Sons, 2016.

Lencioni, Patrick M. *The Motive: Why So Many Leaders Abdicate Their Most Important Responsibilities.* Hoboken, NJ: John Wiley and Sons, 2020.

Lewis, James P. *Working Together: 12 Principles for Achieving Excellence in Managing Projects, Teams, and Organizations.* Washington, DC: BeardBooks, 2006.

Luenendonk, Martin. "11 Leadership Lessons From Napoleon." *Cleverism* (July 25, 2020), http://www.cleverism.com/11-leadership-lessons-from-Napoleon-Bonaparte.

Maister, David. H., *True Professionalism: The Courage to Care About Your People, Your Clients, and Your Career.* New York: Simon and Schuster, 1997.

Maxwell, John C. *The Leader's Greatest Return: Attracting, Developing, and Multiplying Leaders.* United States of America: Harper Collins Leadership, 2020.

Mind Tools Content Team. "Professionalism: Meeting the Standards That Matter." *MindTools,* http://www.mindtools.com/pages/article/professionalism.htm.

Moreland, R. L., and John M. Levine. "Group dynamics over time: Development and socialization in small groups. In J. E. McGrath (Ed.) *The social psychology of time: New perspectives* (pp. 151-181). Newbury Park, CA: Sage Publications, 1988.

Moreland, R. L., and J. M. Levine, (1992). The composition of small groups. *Advances in Group Processes,* 9, 237-280.

Morin, Amy. ""13 Things Mentally Strong People Don't Do." New York: HarperCollins Publishers, 2014

Nooyi, Indra. *My Life in Full: Work, Family, and Our Future.* United States of America: Penguin Random House, 2021.

O'Connor, Carol. *Secrets of Great Leaders: 50 Ways to Make a Difference.* United Kingdom: Quercus, 2015.

Paycor. *Lunch Break Laws by State (2020),* www.paycor.com.

Ogbevoen, Nehi, *What are Microaggressions and How do they Affect Us?.* PCSO Bulletin, (pp. 66-67). Summer 2022.

Stoltz, Bernie. *The Fortune Recipe.* Austin, Texas: Houndstooth Press, 2022.

Strafel, Eric. *The Frontline CEO: Turn Employees into Decision Makers Who Innovate Solutions, Win Customers, and Boost Profits.* New York: McGraw Hill, 2022.

White, Dr. Paul. *The Vibrant Workplace: Overcoming the Obstacles to Building a Culture of Appreciation.* Chicago: Northerfield Publishing, 2017.

Willet, Alan. *Leading the Unleadable: How to Manage Mavericks, Cynics, Divas, and Other Difficult People.* New York: AMACOMbooks, 2016.

Zweifel, Thomas D. *Communicate or Die: Getting Results Through Speaking and Listening.* New York: SelectBooks, 2003.

Zweifel, Dr. Thomas D. *Leadership in 100 Days: Your Systematic Self-Coaching Roadmap to Power and Impact—and Your Future.* New York: iHorizon, 2019.

Zweifel, Dr. Thomas D and Edward J. Borey. *Strategy-In-Action: Marrying Planning, People and Performance.* New York: iHorizon, 2013

INDEX

OTHER BOOKS BY
DR. ANN MARIE GORCZYCA

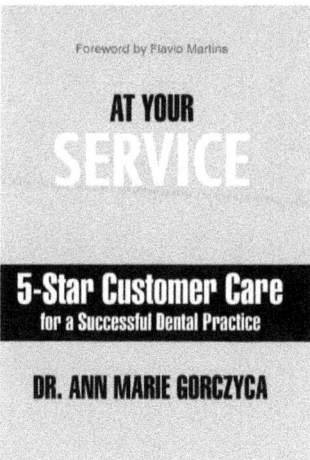

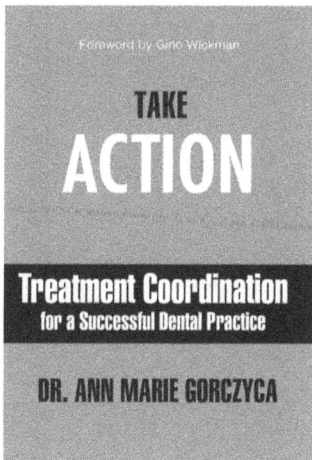

Foreword by Fred Joyal

It All Starts with
MARKETING

201 Marketing Tips
for Growing a Dental Practice

DR. ANN MARIE GORCZYCA

Foreword by Bruce Tulgan

Beyond the Morning
HUDDLE

HR Management
for a Successful Dental Practice

DR. ANN MARIE GORCZYCA

Foreword by Flavio Martins

AT YOUR
SERVICE

5-Star Customer Care
for a Successful Dental Practice

DR. ANN MARIE GORCZYCA

Foreword by Gino Wickman

TAKE
ACTION

Treatment Coordination
for a Successful Dental Practice

DR. ANN MARIE GORCZYCA